CHASING BLISS

*****

A Layman's Guide to Love, Fulfillment,
Damage Control, Repair and Resurrection

By Larry Brooks

CHASING BLISS. Copyright © 2016 by Larry Brooks. All rights reserved. Manufactured in the United States of America. No other part of this book may be reproduced in any form or by an electronic or mechanical means including information storage and retrieval systems without permission in writing from the publisher/author, except by a reviewer, who may quote brief passages in a review. Published by Storyfix.com, 10015 E. Mountain View Road, Suite 1037, Scottsdale, AZ, 85258. (503) 799-9343

www.chasingblissbook.com

Cover design by Praveen.

ISBN: 978-0-9835030-4-0

The author makes no warranties relative to the content or principles described herein, and is not liable for any claims resulting from misuse of this information. The author makes no claim to any academic or professional accreditation in this field, and recommends the involvement of professional counsel in the event of relationship issues.

Special thanks to the authors of the Forewords, Dr. Carrie Rubin and Dr. Marci Nemhauser. To Sue Coletta for her hours of wise contribution. And to Laura, for her years of doing the same.

For Laura...
Who taught me everything.

For Nelson...
She's out there, buddy. Be ready.

For Tracy, Scott, and Kelly...
Always rooting for you. Hope this helps.

Contents

Foreword 1
Foreword 2 4
Introduction 6
Part One: A Wake Up Call For Women 19
Ten Reasons He's Going To Cheat On You 21

    Reason #10: You married your father. 27

    Reason #9: Too much drama 37

    Reason #8: You can't, or won't, give him what he says he needs 40

    Reason #7: The bait worked. The switch didn't 43

    Reason #6: You already left him… for your kids… for your job… or because of your own despair 45

    Reason #5: Mr. Johnson has left the building 47

    Reason #4: You think talk is cheap 50

    Reason #3: Then again, it's really about more than just his sexual needs 52

    Reason #2: No blood, no foul 54

    Reason #1: His moral compass couldn't find North if it had a picture of Santa on it. 57

Part Two: A Wake-Up Call* For Men 61
Ten Reasons She's Going To Leave You 63

    Reason #10: You equate sex with orgasms 69

Reason #9: You are tone deaf to the music of your co-existence 75

Reason #8: Your conflict resolution skills suck 80

Reason #7: It's all about you 83

Reason #6: Your dark side trumps your many charms ... 87

Reason #5: You… the dream that never came true 91

Reason #4: Once best friends, now roommates 94

Reason #3: She no longer trusts you 96

Reason #2: She no longer respects you 99

Reason #1: The phenomenon of *snap*. 101

Part Three: The Domestic Warrior's Tool* Chest 109

Five Case Studies in the Blame Game 111

1. You don't recognize that guy behind the wheel. And you don't like him, either 114

2. Oh *that*? It's just his little "thing." 116

3. Seize the weekend. Yours, not his 118

4. Communicate, don't triangulate 120

5. The best defense is a good, well, defense 122

Realms of Relationship 125

1. The Realm of Safety 127

2. The Realm of Authenticity 134

3. The Realm of Inner Demons 141

4. The Realm of Tone 151

5. The Languages of Love 159

6. The Realm of Conflict Resolution 163

7. The Realm of Romance, Sex and Intimacy 176

8. The Realm of the Everyday.. 190
The Everyday Playbook of Bliss..................................203
The Tough Questions... 221
Epilogue..225
From The Author's Wife..233
About the Authors..236

Foreword
by Carrie Rubin, M.D.

We all have lightbulb moments where something we see or read or hear starts us on a new trajectory. For me, one of those moments was when I discovered Larry's books on the craft of writing. His approach to story structure in *Story Engineering* changed the way I write, making plot holes and writer's block a thing of the past.

As if that weren't reward enough, I later got to know Larry through social media and found him to be genuine, down-to-earth, and blessed with common sense. In other words, he tells it like it is and logically connects point A to point B. So when Larry asked me to write a Foreword for his nonfiction book on relationships, I was both honored and thrilled. I knew his book would come from the heart and contain helpful real-life advice.

I was not disappointed.

As a physician, I've watched many couples interact over the years in various emotional settings. I've also read a great deal on human behavior. And, like Larry, I've been happily married for over 20 years. As such, my interest in *Chasing Bliss: A Layman's Guide to Love, Fulfillment, Damage Control, Repair and Resurrection* is both professional and personal.

Furthermore, I'm a realist and pragmatist, so I was delighted to see *Chasing Bliss* follows the same direct style as Larry's writing books. Within its insightful pages, you will find a tell-it-like-it-is guide on how to make your relationship work. No endless recitation of studies, no textbook dryness, no Frasier-Crane lingo—just an entertaining yet serious discussion on the ways we sabotage our relationships and how we can fix them.

And the cherry on top? Larry knows of what he speaks. He's been there himself. After two failed marriages, he finally found marital success, and as he explains in the book, that success "doesn't involve settling or even accepting the inevitable challenges of being married."

Larry doesn't hold back, and that's what makes this book an absorbing read. When he promises to tell us the ten reasons men will cheat and how eight of them have to do with the woman, we sit up and listen! Larry also vows to reveal "the stuff you wish someone—your partner, your shrink, someone—would just say to you, rather than put you through the emotional ringer to figure it out for yourself." On that promise he delivers, making the purpose of this book helping us push our relationship beyond one that's merely fine to one that's leaning into bliss.

Divided into three parts, the first section addresses women and what they can do to better meet their partners' needs; the second addresses men's issues, many of which stem from speaking a different emotional language than their partner; and the third addresses both sexes, offering a tool chest that looks at the primary realms of relationships. How we navigate them—including how well we own up to our own behaviors—is what sinks us or moves us closer to bliss.

But don't worry about generalized gender assumptions. Larry is quick to point out how risky that can be. Some women may relate more to the men's section and vice versa. He only divides the two genders because stereotypes often carry some truth, and for any advice to be helpful, it must be realistic and relatable. Indeed, plenty of crossover between the sexes exists—part of the challenge is that some people try to live into their own perception of gender expectations when that may actually be counter-productive—and for that reason, I advise readers to take all the guidelines to heart. You never know where you might find a wake-up call in regards to your own behavior.

As both a professional and a wife, I've always felt the keys to a happy, sustained relationship are communication, respect, and a sense of humor. Larry breaks these elements down even further into trust, respect, safety, hope, and joy, stating that the quality of this "five-ingredient stew is the determinant of which direction [the relationship] goes." Implicit in these fundamental ingredients is the need to invest in and nurture our relationship to meet our partner's needs, even if those needs differ from our own. It is this self-awareness, leading to selflessness, that Larry wants us to achieve, because only when we look in the mirror first can we start a journey toward relationship bliss.

One final caveat: the beauty of this book is its power to be a tool for both relationship recovery and healthy relationship maintenance. For those in good shape, its advice will serve as a protective life vest, one that will keep you from sinking into troubled waters. Because, as Larry sums up in one of my favorite lines of the book: "Some toothpaste just can't be stuffed back into the tube."

Carrie Rubin, MD, MPH
May 2016

Foreword 2
by Marci Nemhauser, PsyD, PCC

When Larry asked me if I would be willing to write an introduction to this book, I was both surprised and flattered. Larry and I met, along with his wife Laura, several years ago. We happened to all be on a quest to find additional meaning and purpose in our lives. It was a special and delightful interaction!

I am a licensed Psychologist and Executive Coach and have my own business. Larry and Laura were seeking new ways to build their business and explore new realms of personal growth. We had much to talk about.

One of the impressions I left our first meeting with is the way they interacted as a couple. I liked the easy give and take between them. It was evident that they liked each other.

So I wasn't totally surprised to receive this book about relationships based on Larry's evolution as a partner, husband, and lover. But I also had to "walk back" my initial reaction to a "man telling women what we need to know." At first, at least for me, Larry's light-hearted style was confusing to the message he was trying to impart. But as I read on, I began to see that message and understand what he was trying to convey.

As a Psychologist who has worked with many couples, I know the minefield that can be created in relationships over time. There is a psychological term called "the bi-personal field" that was coined by Robert Langs, MD. It is the interconnection that is created by the couple and becomes a kind of entity in and of itself. I used this image and pictured the couple being in a dance within that field. Nothing would change if both didn't fully engage in the process.

As Larry articulates with humor and insight, he conveys this form of dance occurring within a relationship. He has put a male voice to many of the questions women have wanted to understand. (Parenthetically, let me emphasize that understanding is not the same as condoning or accepting behaviors, rationales or excuses… sometimes understanding can lead to the exact opposite result. Larry does not condone or rationalize the negative with a context of gender, but rather, suggests that we harness a higher understanding of who we are within a relationship to create positive change and the elevation of the relationship as a result.)

I also found the section at the end about the Warrior's Tool Chest a useful reminder for everyone in any type of relationship. Being willing to hold yourself accountable to your own promises lends authenticity and credibility to your request for others to do the same. We all want to feel admired, respected, loved and honored. In order to receive those things, we need to first face our own fears, doubts and worry about our worthiness. It is easy to see the problem *out there*, but looking *inward* is the way to find the path to creating a loving, authentic relationship that grows stronger over time.

Larry's book is a good beginning to that journey.

Marci Nemhauser, PsyD, PCC
July 2015

Introduction

I love my wife. Desperately.

That particular adjective—*desperately*—among others that I could just as validly apply in its place, speaks volumes about our relationship. It both implies and defines the give-and-take between us while putting a fence around what either of us can live with in terms of the other being less than perfect.

Which happens frequently.

All of us, by the way, have that same fence. Sometimes high and unforgiving, sometimes full of holes, sometimes torn down altogether and trampled beneath the weight of regret. This dance is an unassailable fact of life in every primary relationship, even when *desperate* doesn't apply.

My wife does not love me desperately. She makes that abundantly clear whenever we talk about this, which we often do. She loves me *unconditionally*. I asked her—it's not my place to decide how she loves me, from her point of view—and this was the word she chose.

Unconditionally. A loaded word, that.

Because, while I grasp and appreciate the intention of that response, she actually doesn't love me unconditionally. There are limits in our —and any—relationship. As there should be, because those limits are what set standards of respect and commitment, two of several essential relationship variables.

By definition, limits imply consequences. If I cheated on her, for example, she assures me she would plant a two-by-four squarely in the middle of my forehead while I sleep, and that it would be a committed swing the likes of which Barry Bonds would have been proud.

That's something other than unconditional. And, I suspect, not an exclusively metaphoric description of what would happen should I ever cross that line. Happily for us both, we are not at risk in this regard, and not remotely because of that threat.

Rather, we remain viable because the fire still burns. Due in no small part to what we know about relationship maintenance and the pursuit of marital bliss, and seek to share in this little book. And what we do in the light of that knowledge when challenges arise.

Then again, while she may still love me in such a dark circumstance, nonetheless that piece of lumber, like the transgression that (hypothetically) instigated it, would change everything. Because she also assures me she would throw me out on my sorry ass if this ever happens. Right after I am let out of the hospital. No second chances.

My wife has a high level of respect for herself, a view shared by all who know her. I share that esteem for her, and this becomes an important note in our dance (some wryly suggest that I actually fear her—I get that—but it's just a perception).

The proposition of the two-by-four and the ensuing ejection from her life are not threats. They are consequences, either metaphorically or literally. And they are totally, if not a bit extreme, reasonable.

There are always consequences. That's the point here.

The good news is that the consequences cut both ways. Which means that the good and loving efforts we make, even if they seem to go unacknowledged in the moment, come back to us in mysterious and beautiful ways.

Where we lose our way is when we forget that this applies to the inevitable lesser transgressions common to cohabitation, or even those things that simply lack proper maintenance. You forget to oil your car, and after a while there are consequences. Odd sounds and alarming odors from under the hood ensue. Same with being in love.

I don't require fear or threats to dissuade me from temptation.

Just as the death penalty has been proven to have absolutely no pre-emptive effect on the murder rate, fear isn't—in my case, at least—what keeps temptation or weakness at bay. It's not fear of that two-by-four that keeps me home and focused on this amazing, stunning, powerful woman. Rather, it is a beautiful and totally unforced amalgamation of things, beginning with pure and passionate love that has been honed, tested and reinforced over time. With time has come a fortified commitment and sense of respect—for her and for myself, as well as for the assurances we've given to each other—and the wisdom to know what this means, which comes with life experience.

Over time, life softens the edges, bleeds gray into the black and white of logic and limits, and it leads toward prioritization and the solidification of values. All that strength and fierceness and the certainly of consequences… that's absolutely part of the chemistry that fascinates me about her.

She makes me a better husband, a better father, a better man.

She also makes me crazy sometimes. It's part of the deal, and fundamental to the pursuit of bliss. Perfection is not the point—it never has been—so let's not confuse it with bliss. That level of sheer happiness arrives in a moment, and it can depart in one. Such an awareness is critical. True bliss is the sum of our moments and the aggregated scent of the air between us. When we expect perfection, and moreover, when we react harshly when things aren't perfect, we are taking a step backward in what is always, as a best-case scenario, a two-steps-forward-one-step-back dance.

Understanding that is bliss in itself. It creates the space we need to be less than perfect, while not remotely licensing it. Like love, bliss is paradoxical in that regard.

I know how lucky I am to have her. Sometimes, when we are with friends or engaged in something other than conversing, I catch myself just staring at her (this happens a lot in the soft light of a movie theater), lost in her beauty, amazed at the nuances and depth of her passion and joy and comprehension, and her capacity for love on so many levels. It is then that I am reminded how deeply in love I am, and how the work, sometimes very hard, is worth the effort. It is the work, as much as the woman herself, that makes me a better person, and imbues my marriage with an awareness that it is the primary journey of my life, along with being a father. In these arenas, while never completely attainable, perfection should always be the goal.

Our two decades of marital success—the bottom line sum of it all—doesn't involve settling or even accepting the inevitable challenges of being married. Rather, our success resides in doing just the opposite. We embrace the challenges, we learn from them, we even value them.

And we never settle for *normal*.

Because bliss, which is the goal, is not normal.

At the end of the day we hold each other accountable, which leads to understanding and, when called for, growth.

This isn't my first marriage, nor is it hers.

And like my wife, I've learned how to be successful in a relationship the old fashioned way: through self-reflection born of pain, juxtaposed more with the consequences of dishing it than experiencing it. Pain becomes an acid test of love, when the prospect of infliction defines the nature of the give and take of a relationship.

When the certainty or even the possibility of hurting her is on the table, love defines what happens next. And there is no hiding from that outcome. Every partner who has ever considered crossing a line, or speaking harshly without deeper thought, has forgotten what is important and expected perfection in an imperfect proposition, has faced this choice. The primary goal of this book is to help you choose wisely and fully informed.

You might think that the fact of my being married twice before disqualifies me from writing this book. But I argue the exact opposite is true. Everything you are about to read is the product of our collective life experience, which, in my case, includes a few semesters in the school of relationship hard knocks and a few more in the penalty box for being a schmuck, otherwise known as being a typical guy.

She assures me I am not a typical guy, despite slinging that arrow when I fall into one of the many typical guy traps. Which I do.

There, I said it. It's true, I do believe men—many men, not all—have a higher mountain to climb than do women. Most women, that is. As the lyrics to a preponderance of both country and pop songs testify, there are more than a few certifiable emotional psychopaths out there without penises, as well.

A few friends who know I am a novelist and also know that I am writing this book have suggested that I am moved to do so as a result of writing about love and relationships in my fiction, where I dive deeply into the complexities—often dark, because that can make for a whopper of a story—of what works and what doesn't, and what can come of testing either ceiling. And yes, more than a few of my female characters are fierce and uncompromising.

Such is how life informs our art.

I write relationship thrillers because of my fascination with the eternal and age-old dance between lovers and partners, and the vulnerabilities this creates. And thus, this book becomes the most important thing I have ever endeavored to put onto paper.

I've been through more than one counseling experience, and I've read a shelf full of books on the subject of primary relationships. Other than context, none of that wisdom is simply being repeated here. All of it, however, informs what I'm about to share, which is an interpretation of and for real life, with a clear perspective on the consequences that stem from our choices. This is, by intention, the stuff you wish someone—your partner, your shrink, someone—would just say to you, rather than put you through the emotional ringer to figure out for yourself.

"You tell me," says the shrink when you pose a question that is carving a hole in your heart. I am here to try to do just that. Not as an academic, but as an experienced player on that field. One who, while being far from perfect at it, has been paying attention, taking notes, testing theories and compiling a significant mountain of research that has been witnessed and lived firsthand.

Let me say it again: there are always consequences. Which means, precisely because of this certainty, to a huge extent we get to choose our outcomes.

Marriage is hard. Always.

Time is the enemy, because without management it leads to apathy, atrophy, resentment, laziness and the ultimate relegation of control over your relationship to autopilot status, which is the Great Killer of love stories. These things conspire to create an environment that is the most toxic of all possible relationship dynamics: the loss of hope.

And thus the divorce lawyers are all getting rich on the backs of the broken.

Battling those forces is the key to success. Recognition of them is the first step in that battle.

Allow me to say that again: *autopilot* is the enemy.

The destroyer of bliss, or any shot at it. You may have thought it was tension, the day-to-day drama of it all, but usually tension can be traced back to autopilot. In his book *People of the Lie*, the late M. Scott Peck (his earlier book, *The Road Less Traveled*, was one of my first life wake-up calls, and a book I highly recommend) postulates that all human evil and darkness can be traced back to the consequences of laziness. This applies to primary relationships, as well, because autopilot is the essence of laziness.

If you've ever forgotten an anniversary or birthday, you know this to be true. And that consequences cannot be avoided.

If you've ever withheld expressing a frustration, some feedback or downright anger because you didn't want to do the work of dealing with the response—perhaps defending that decision because you know the sh*t-storm it would cause—you have been guilty of this laziness, seasoned with a dose of self-justifying cowardice.

We humans are strange beasts. We tend to take for granted that which is most important to us. And often, deteriorating right under our noses. We too easily accept the consequences of silence to avoid the hard work and often painful outcome of forthright honesty. For which there is a time and a place, commencing a dialogue driven by sensitivity and common sense.

Sooner or later a relationship—any relationship—needs maintenance and refueling. Like an airplane or a bird, it needs to land on something, and a landing never happens on autopilot. Marriage is the truest case study I can imagine for the adage: *if you're not moving forward, you are dying*. In marriage or any primary relationship, while it may feel like you're dying, more often it first feels like you're stagnant, perhaps bored and, soon thereafter, disappointed. Which is too often the precursor of relationship problems, if not the outright trigger for them.

You need to summon the courage and means to confront it all before it is, without warning, more powerful than you. Relationship erosion—the dilution of sexual and domestic chemistry, simmered with resentment, apathy and laziness—reaches a point, I believe, where it becomes irreversible. Where something has truly been lost. Or at least, where it inflicts damage that cannot be undone, usually with words that cannot be unheard. Scars can be lived with, but some wounds are deep enough to puncture an artery and, over time, bleed out.

Everything may indeed be fine in your primary relationship.

You may accept that, over time, things change (they certainly do), that the raging fire you once knew has become an acceptably warm ember. Maybe just a lump of coal. But for me, and perhaps for you, as well, fine isn't good enough. Bliss is a possible dream, and the very pursuit of it, from an informed perspective, is what can save, heal, resurrect and otherwise empower your primary relationship.

If, rather than the destination, it is the nature of the journey that defines success in life's struggles, then within a primary relationship it is effort, rather than complete efficacy, that becomes the thing to focus on.

Bliss is a noble but lofty goal to pursue.

It resists, it is elusive, it must be fought for. You have to chase it. Engage in the struggle for it. Be vulnerable to it. Be willing to change for it. The pursuit of primary relationship bliss is the greatest adventure a human being can experience. It—the pursuit itself—can be the greatest gift you can give to your partner, not to mention to yourself.

Because even with great effort, things will never be completely ideal. Stuff happens, always. The mantra "marriage is hard" is constantly reinforced by our reality. But the margin for error and forgiveness is always more liberal when the ship is moving forward, at least when you are both committed to it. Because that forward motion translates to hope, and hope is the fuel for everything where bliss is concerned.

For me, this journey is defined by a fact: my wife is a high-spirited, often impatient and highly focused woman. On her darkest days, she is textbook high maintenance, something she owns completely, thus allowing me to say it here. (On my darkest days, I'm a textbook guy, which is worse.) Sometimes her focus isn't on *me*. On the other hand, as I've said, I am desperately in love with her—literally—for reasons that go way back and in some ways have as much to do with my inner demons and the backstory that created them than they do with her. Nonetheless, this results in my almost always being focused on her, if not directly then within a heartbeat, and thus, expecting too much, too intensely, too often.

Something she calls *needy*.

I, too, am high maintenance in that regard.

We are all, in one way or another, high maintenance.

To expect our partners to think and act as we would, and to respond without considerable deliberation before doing so, is one of the most toxic attributes of the climate of a love story in jeopardy.

We are very different, my wife and I.

But we share one key thing, among many things, that makes it all work: we are equally committed to this journey, to the effort, heading toward the discovery, delivery and appreciation of bliss, all within a context of accepting, forgiving and healing our respective imperfections while hovering over the safety net of respect.

That paragraph contains a checklist that always serves us.

The loss of respect is a sure-thing a relationship killer, right up there with erosion stemming from lack of care, which in turn leads to a loss of hope. When hope is lost, you are toast. Whatever the symptoms, whatever the story, a failing relationship almost always has this on the menu.

What you are about to read is the learning we have discovered and shared. Tested and forged. Both from our 20-plus years together, and from the battered backstories we bring to them.

This material is presented in three parts.

One for women, one for men, and one for both. This is not exclusive of non-traditional partnerships, by the way. Because like love itself, those role paradigms exist in virtually any union.

That said, the intention is not to exclude either gender from any of these three parts. In fact, there is great value in men reading the section optimized for women, and vice versa.

Getting into the head of your partner is not just a strategy, it can be a means of survival.

The third part of this book is a tool chest that applies to both sides of the relationship, regardless of gender or the roles you have assumed. Here is where we break the relationship down into various and inevitable facets—which I refer to as realms, because we live in them on a daily basis—any one of which can be a deal breaker, and all of which experience the erosion of time and the wear and tear of living with a partner who doesn't completely and consistently get it, which is often a simultaneous feeling on both sides. Awareness of who you are within each realm can lead to a clearer interpretation of who your partner is, as well, empowering both of you to take your union to a higher place, one realm at a time.

My wish is that you find something here to work with.

To acknowledge and to embrace. That you might step into the abyss that is the search for bliss with trust in your love, and in your courage to see it through. Whether you act on these principles or not, you will need both.

The highest form of love and heroism is to be there for your spouse or partner, truly in good times and in bad. The goal here is to shine a light on where you are, and clear the path to where you would like to be. And perhaps, where you need to be, as well.

That last one might challenge you, and it might surprise you. I hope it does, and that you can see yourself in that place.

May you find hope, possibly even bliss, when it happens. Because, as I've knowingly said twice before thus far, and will most certainly say again, hope is the lifeblood of true and enduring happiness.

With hope still alive, anything can be accomplished.

It is doable. And as cliché as it sounds, the journey really is the point. The good news is, once the race is entered, you don't have to go it alone.

At the very least, I hope this book gives you and your spouse or partner something to talk about.

Larry Brooks
June 2016

Part One

A Wake-Up Call*
For Women

(*Good to know, too, if you're a man living with one.)

Ten Reasons He's Going To Cheat On You

After reading these, you may not be able to say you didn't see it coming.

It's always risky to put people into little metaphoric boxes, especially relationship-based boxes, because there are always exceptions that will make you wrong. This is true with or without a penis, by the way, there are boxes that apply to all of us. But here's a metaphoric box that, while statistically irrelevant and otherwise virtually impossible to prove, very few people will challenge. At least those who have been there. It's not an absolute, but it *is* a truism. And when it comes to the breakdown of a primary relationship—i.e., who cheats, who leaves, who doesn't, and why—it illuminates a fundamental difference between men and women:

Men generally leave women for another woman.

Women generally leave men for another life.

This is less a mantra for those who cheat than it is for the outcome of cheating gone terribly wrong. Because women cheat, too, and often for the exact same reasons. But even so, when a woman cheats it usually tends to prove these propositions. They cheat for the experience, both emotional and physical, rather than to appease an appetite.

Husbands tend to cheat to get laid, and then lie to themselves about why, that it meant something. Then lie again when they tell their partner, when they're caught at it, that it didn't mean anything at all.

It is the question of the cause of the effect relative to cheating that links back to a deeper, more disturbing question, more than the moral fiber of the transgressor.

One of the first and biggest mistakes women make in attempting to understand why their men cheat on them, or want to cheat on them (which is nearly as devastating and far more frequent), is to try to apply the same rationale you would use if temptation crossed your own mind. Which may actually happen, however briefly.

And therein resides the making of emotional chaos. Because if you try to explain your man's behavior from the point of view of a woman, you're getting nowhere fast.

Because his life might be just fine, all things considered. And, he still might cheat on you.

Almost always—unless she's a frisky little exception herself—when a woman cheats it's a step toward moving on with her life, or at least escaping it for a while, leaving her dumbfounded man behind to sort it all out in a sea of tears and beer. Sure, women have been known to have one-nighters and the occasional secret online virtual fling, but for the most part that's an episode of *Girls* on HBO.

This, by the way, is the reason romance novels consistently outsell all other genres by a wide margin. They deliver a safe and vicarious escape, not at all unlike the rationale men provide for looking at porn. We all have needs, and that very thing resides at the core of why either side cheats, whatever form that takes.

Truth is, women tend to cheat for *love* and an illusion of romance more than they cheat for fun (some women assure me they are as shallow and horny as the men they live with). Guys, on the other hand, tend to truly believe they do it for reasons that are complex, but with closer scrutiny are as transparent as their cover stories. Reasons that are easier to predict. But because those reasons defy the emotional logic a woman brings to the proposition—men being in 24-7 defiance of emotional logic beginning at the age of 13—and because any issues at the core of their betrayal are often (likely) of their own making, they can be challenging to prevent.

While there are ten reasons for his cheating offered here, they may be tricky to wrap your head around because of two overriding principles that inform all ten.

First principle: all ten of these reasons he might cheat on you can lead to the same outcome: *infidelity*, in some form (an affair of the heart counts, by the way), usually followed by the loss of a vital body part.

By the time he's been caught with his pants down, or his heart broken, the lines between those reasons will have blurred, one quickly and seamlessly begetting another. Before long you aren't really sure which of these ten infuriating excuses apply.

Almost always, several will.

But if you look closely enough, and quickly enough before he steps over the line, you can break these reasons, and the vicious circle within which they dance, down into their component parts and see what's behind them. When you get clear on what's eating at him, or pulling him away, or where he is simply broken. That's when you'll find ten different boxes into which to put these reasons for his cheating. And then, perhaps, bury them.

Into which bodily orifice this takes place is entirely up to you.

Second principle: these ten reasons break down into two categories, which become chapter headings for more specific symptoms of impending sliminess. His cheating is either:

1.) because of you, at least to some extent—and there are eight of these excuses here—or…
2.) it has very little, if anything at all, to do with you.

Which means it has everything to do with him.

Many women would like to force-feed their sad victim story into the latter category. But the truth is, it usually has something to do with you after all. Even just a little bit.

But don't overreact. This is not to say it's *all* your fault. Or even mostly your fault. What it means is, the reason your guy steps out will have an explanation behind it, however lame and totally of his creation, a reason he's unhappy or restless, and by definition that includes you. A rationale. Your marriage may seem perfect to you, but it may be lacking for him.

In other words, your perfect may not be his perfect.

More than one philandering guy has stepped out on a perfectly lovely, wonderful woman because his desire is for a woman, even for a night, who has the moral compass of a sociopath and the sexual appetite of a closet succubus. In other words, he desires to experience some combination of fantasy and the sense that he is living large. He actually wants to be used, even abused, to just as likely, be the user— whatever that might mean to him.

There is a major hotel in Las Vegas with the tagline, *"Just the right amount of wrong."* It is the wise woman who can read her man and deliver on that from time to time.

And before you ring the misogyny bell, rest assured, I believe that to be true for men, as well. When both sides of that equation flip the genders of that sentence and go there from time to time, bliss is even more attainable.

Defending the Indefensible

By all means, his rationale for stepping out might be completely unreasonable, which means everyone still gets to take your side when the bleeding begins. But because you're involved, however tangentially, it's always good to understand what's going on for him that might lead to suspicious lipstick smudges.

Of course, there's always the guy who cheats simply because he *can*. Because he can't not cheat. It's his nature. He believes it's his birthright, as long as he can get away with it. A purebred, this guy.

He's truly a cad, a cardboard cutout of a man, and that's a problem you can't remedy no matter how hard you try. That bad boy you thought you could fix… sorry, not gonna happen. You may corral him for a while, but with time comes the erosion of the gates that keep him home. His ego, his need for the reassurance that comes with another woman's touch, is bigger than his love for you. He won't see it that way, of course, which adds a layer of psychosis to the mix that might be bigger than both of you. Which means you'll need the help of a professional to get through this.

Such rationale is an inescapable fact of people of either gender who cannot handle the truth, hidden beneath the pile of paradoxical rationalization labeled: *if I thought I'd get caught I'd have never done it, because I would never hurt you.*

Everyone will be on your side then, too.

But being a self-serving, insensitive, morally bankrupt, self-deluding liar is only one of these ten reasons, and one of two that exempt you from accountability.

Let's begin with the others, where you at least stand a chance to make a difference.

One final note before we dig in.

By cheating, I'm referring to your partner's opting for a wrong and destructive choice, despite it being an obvious violation of the agreement between you, both implied and legal and moralistic. Tough times between you don't license cheating, they are simply the rationale of the guilty.

It's not just stepping out with someone else, either. Cheating could mean a preference for alcohol or drugs over you. Or pornography. Or the infliction of abuse, emotional and physical, because that cheats on the expectation you shared. Or simply disappearing from the emotional landscape. While these may not feel like he's stepping out, the degree to which you rationalize these as not stepping away from you is the degree to which you need to look deeper for true understanding

Existing within a primary relationship is never simple, never mind being easy. Which means the vehicle of his indiscretion is as subject to this analysis as any other.

The same goes for taking responsibility for it.

Here then, in receding order, are the ten reasons he might cheat on you.

Reason #10: You married your father.

Allow me to use this one as a sort of catch-all leading to your response to these various causal factors. Things get generic—perhaps universal is the better term here—because unhappy is unhappy, communications voids and dysfunction apply to them all, and the calling for a healthy and productive response, one not informed by revenge or punishment, is always before you.

That said, let's talk about one of the biggies first. The younger you are, the younger you were when you opted-in to this relationship, or your first one (because it's good to understand what went wrong there, too), the greater the odds of this one applying to you.

You married your father. And you may not even know it.

Your father may be/have been a great guy.

Everybody loves (or loved) him because he is/was funny and generous, perhaps successful, a good provider, for all intents and purposes a family man. And he was a good father to you.

Conversely, your father may have been a poster boy for what I call DGS (Dumb Guy Syndrome). Or worse, a complete lout.

But who he was is not the issue, relative to what a man and a good-to-great mate needs to be for you now. Let's get real and be clear: a great father does not a great husband/partner make, and vice versa.

The issue is that, as a little girl, you idolized the father that you and everybody else loved. Or not, as his little girl you might have been a majority of one in the column of those who loved and respected your father.

Either way, this affection can come back to bite you, if you knowingly or unknowingly fell for someone that reminded you of your father. Because your father was not your lover. Or let us hope that's the case.

Or just as frequently, in looking for a partner you yearned for a level of approval and attention that always seemed to come up short in your childhood, particularly from your father. Maybe he favored your brother by a wide and obvious margin. But even through that fog, you began to define manhood itself through his example, using the limited peripheral vision of a child.

You were a little girl. Those imprints on your subconscious were less than fully mature, less than evolved, and completely naïve. You had no idea what it meant for a man (or a partner) to be a good husband, or even a good man in general. You had—and likely still have—no idea at all what kind of lover and partner your father was. Or maybe you do, and it was toxic. Either way, you had little to nothing from which to judge or compare the gender roles your parents lived into, at least in those years when your subconscious mind was taking notes.

You couldn't possibly comprehend the qualitative nature of the husband he was (versus what kind of father he was), which is the issue. You only lived one side of the reality of the man, which was experienced, internalized and judged through the lens of a child. In the long list of ways that men can fall off a pedestal, love for their child is usually the last thing to go.

And so, in spite of everything, he still loved you. And you want more of that kind of love.

Often there's a significant difference between a man as a mate and the same man as a father.

And the difference can come back at you if, either subconsciously or on purpose, you allowed the imprint of your father's representation of manhood and husband-hood to influence who you selected as a mate.

You probably didn't think about it in these terms. You found a guy, you were attracted to him, and here you are. One day you wake up and realize—or not—that you are married to your father.

And suddenly the echo of your mother's misery begins to make sense.

Your father might have been a saint on all fronts.

Then again, behind closed doors, when engaged in conflict, he might have been a domestic dinosaur, from a generation or a culture with a value system that doesn't work today. A generation that bred emotional issues for men—indeed, that expected it of them—especially in terms of anger management and the showing of affection. If you end up with a guy who, in retrospect, was your choice because he reminded you of your father, then for better or worse, you're stuck with that choice and the criteria that shaped it.

Chances are your definition of manhood has changed since then.

But odds are you have no idea what your father was really like as a partner. He might have cheated on your mother. He might have beaten her. He might have treated her like the help—*where's my damn dinner, woman?*—and to this day you may not have a clue of this reality. Because a mother's love probably sought to shield you from those dark truths.

29

Or he might have indeed been perfect on all fronts. Those things about him that, because he was your daddy, shaped your definition of manhood—not talking about feelings, obsessive fishing and golfing, an affection for guns, and megalomaniacal control issues and drinking to excess and not wanting to attend family functions and constantly putting your mother down—are often ripples on a deeper pond.

And now you're swimming in it.

This isn't a deal killer.

But to get to the bottom of why your partner is cheating on you, or is simply treating you as *less than*, this dynamic may apply. He is who he is, and you picked him. Some of the things that attracted you to him—a swagger, a bad boy, a party boy, a center of attention, a guy who could talk his way out of or into anything—may actually correlate to what you like about your partner today.

That's probably changed since then. Maybe in ways of which you aren't totally aware.

The primary reason men cheat, then and now: *they're not happy*. They're not full, not complete. There's an emptiness inside of him that you can't fill, and he can't wrap his head around it to an extent necessary to let you fully in.

Maybe if you understood the source and nature of that emptiness, you could work with it to create something different. Rage and tears aren't always the most productive tools in that process, however justified.

The next most likely reason: deep inside, beneath all the testosterone-soaked smokin-and-jokin' joviality and proficiency with a putter and a hammer and a fly rod and a handgun, he has double standards. At the end of an honest day, just possibly, he's simply broken.

That, too, is more common than you can imagine.

The primary reason(s) men aren't happy—well, pick one.

There are too many to count. They may be unhappy with you. Or with your marriage. Or with the concept of marriage in general. Or at least unhappy with the part of marriage that has to do with orgasms. Unhappy at work. Unhappy with themselves. Unhappy with the other political party. Or just plain unhappy by nature, because that's how men are, in his view, which was likely cultivated in part by his own father. Like Tim McGraw sang, sometimes he just wakes up fightin' mad. Just like dear old Greatest Generation dad.

Some of this sourcing of melancholy is based on unrealistic expectations—of themselves, of you, from life itself—that may have been shaped by outdated norms of the past. In other words, gender roles as they play into the dynamic of love, romance and cohabitation.

He's a *man*. He's been led to believe you are living in his castle—he may have even tried to convince you of this supposed fact—of which he is King. One doesn't have to wonder for long where he got that.

At this point it doesn't matter that you married (or chose) your father for reasons you don't understand, though it's helpful to at least start to explain how you got here. For better or worse you inherited those reasons, he simply brought them with him into your relationship, wherever they came from.

You may be able to impact these dynamics, you may not. But in either case, if he's unhappy enough, and/or if he's weak or confused or broken enough, he'll consider getting some on the side to ease the pain and fill that empty space.

In his mind, to be a man again.

Otherwise, consider the possibility that you are simply a player in an unfolding drama. Because where there's smoke, there's a hot blond at the bar in need of a light.

The two of your don't get along anymore.

One reason he'll cheat on you (other than he's so full of bullshit he sees the world in shades of brown), is that your marriage sucks, primarily because of that fact. You, on the other hand, are thinking that your marriage sucks because of him, not because of you. Right or wrong, at this point let's just proceed under that assumption.

Either way, this isn't what either of you signed up for. He isn't who you thought he was, or worse, who you think he should be. If you've got any backbone at all, you're delivering a healthy dose of attitude and disapproval right back at him. It's a duel, a face-off, and you'll be damned if you're going to lose. A good old fashioned pissing match disguised as a power struggle. You give as good as you get.

Doesn't take a rocket scientist to realize that this, in turn, is not conducive to steamy sex between you, or even simply getting along. The air you share has a tepid, even foul bouquet. But whether it's the clammy coitus or the bitter waters of your shared existence to blame, he's no longer a happy camper, and when that's the case there's almost always trouble in sex city. He's headed for that bar with a lighter in his pocket.

One common trap is of your own creation, and you stepped into it years ago.

You fell in love with a genuine bad boy, a real James Dean, a bona fide Marlboro man. Or worse—and you might want to check with your mother on this one—you fell in love with a clone of your father, who wasn't the husband you thought he was, because your experience of him relied on other criteria.

Once upon a time that bad boy thing turned you on. It was exciting. The textbook explanation for your choice is that, deep inside, you felt like you could fix him. That he'd abandon his less than evolved, wicked ways just for you.

And perhaps, maintain just enough of it within easy reach, also just for you. He was dangerous, and on a given night still can be.

It was quite an ego trip if you think about it—nobody could tame him until you came along, and by God, he was hot. He gave it all up for you. You tamed the beast. You got the guy no other woman could land (easily mistaken for the guy no other woman wanted). All that imminent danger, the smell of the forbidden, the creaking of black leather on that motorcycle seat, the scent of stale beer and dirty ashtrays on his breath…yeah, what a turn on.

But not anymore.

The bad boy thing got old.

One day you realized you can't fix him. He's no longer a bad boy in your eyes. He's just an incorrigible, self-centered little boy who never grew up. Who doesn't "get it." It's all about him, and always has been.

But guess what: now you do get it. And he knows it. But the thing is, he's completely clueless about how to meet you in the middle, how to change. Or worse, he's done trying to make you happy. He feels rejected, he is who he is and damn proud of it.

Perhaps just like his father. Which is a hard tape to erase.

It might go deeper than that. You were raised with an image of a *real man*. And while your adult self may have since recognized that dear old dad was a dear old wannabe on that front, the programming runs deep. Real men, like dad, like guns and beer and big tits, they don't cry and they don't give a hoot about interior decorating, which is woman's work. They can, like dad, tune the hell out of your car, fix your toilet and spin a good story. And, tune you out in a heartbeat. Real men don't talk much, unless they're telling a joke or flipping someone off. They kill animals for fun (they claim it's for the meat), because that's what real men do, what they have done for thousands of years. They love pastimes and pleasures and vices that you don't, even though you've given them a fair shot.

It's not that these things are inherently bad, even when they are. That's your call. Many wonderful men and partners indulge in all of it.

That's not *it*, though it may be a symptom of it.

Either way, after a while you realize he loves those things more than he loves you. And he doesn't seem to hear you when you ask him to choose you for a change.

He knows what he's risking, because you've told him. But he doesn't change. He doesn't hear you, of if he does, the message is stale by morning. The noise of his inner *guy*, informed by the ghost of his father, is screaming at him to stay in control.

It's just who I am, deal with it.

You wake up one day and admit something that became clear soon after you began to cohabitate: he has the depth of a mud puddle, the moral compass of a sociopath, the awareness (especially of you) of a coma patient, the well-ordered priorities of a nine-year-old, the strength of character of a convicted felon, the conflict resolution skills of a WWE star, the expanding belly of a sumo wrestler, the aroma (not to mention fashion sense) of an old sleeping bag, and the long-term vision of an imprisoned octogenarian serving out a life sentence.

He'd say you're nobody's prize, too. Count on it.

Okay, that's pretty harsh. If your guy reads this and wants to push back on some of those points, that's a good thing. But admit it, some of that is what you feel on your darkest days. The point is...

... there's trouble in river city, and in your mind it's all his fault. Who can blame you, right? His idea of romance is to go clamming at the coast.

Well, guess what: regardless of who is right or wrong, who is the ass and who is the long-suffering martyr, all of this, and your response to it, has effectively killed the ambiance and the sexual tension between you. Love itself is fading, if it's not gone already. And even though it's so obviously not your fault, here's the rub: he may go find it elsewhere. And no one who has spent any amount of time with the two of you will be surprised.

Except you.

Keeping him happy to the point where he won't cheat on you is the least of your problems.

Your first option is to work on your relationship.

On *you* being happy.

That one is key. Let's be clear, the path to an improved relationship is you being truly happy and fulfilled, full of hope as you look forward, rather than faking it as you condescend to his needs. Meeting in the middle where it works, demanding change where it doesn't.

And the first place to look for that, hard as it is, is to go deep inside yourself and ask if, just maybe, you're part of the reason the relationship sucks. Part of the reason, right or wrong, that he'll cheat. Ask if you have the resources, the time, the courage, the clarity and the willingness to do the work it will take to make it all better.

Then pay attention to the answer.

The good news is that, if this is you and the answer to those last questions is *no*, chances are the whole thing will detonate before a domestic Armageddon arrives. Or you'll simply continue to live with compromises. Small consolation, but in that case nothing anybody can say will matter.

A quick note for men reading this section.

You may be feeling a little uneasy right about now. Wondering who this author dude is, coming down on men in general. You'd like a peek at his Man Card to see if it's been punched lately, or maybe just to check if *I've* been punched lately (answer: no). I can see how that's what it might feel like, especially if some of this became a mirror you'd rather not look into.

This is not about men in general. It's about women who married someone who fits into these descriptions, which I challenge you to argue aren't out there. If not you, then I'm betting you know a guy who is a fit for this particular suit.

I mention this to assure you that what's coming next might be more to your liking. Reasons men cheat that aren't merely because they're cheaters at heart, but rather, men who may be *driven* to cheat, or feel as if they are, which is the more likely rationale. Which embraces the role and accountability of the women on the other side of the equation. That mirror, I assure you, will be of equal, unflinching clarity.

It's always a dance for two. Either or both of you chose wrong, for what seemed like good reasons at the time. Or, one or both of you has evolved into someone other than who your partner thought they were getting when they closed the deal.

The mirror doesn't discriminate. And like I said in the Introduction, it takes great courage to look into it and see not only the truth, but your future, as well. That much is equally true for both partners in any relationship.

Reason #9: Too much drama.

In short, you give him a good reason to cheat. At least that's his story.

This is different than the prior reason because it isn't so much about him being an ass, regardless of where that came from. No, with this guy, it's that *you're* the one who is high maintenance these days (and of course, every high maintenance woman on the planet justifies her behavior because her man is lacking, but that's not the point here).

You nag. Doesn't matter that he deserves it, you are still a nag. He can't do anything right. You're no fun anymore. You have control issues. You're never wrong. Meanwhile, you complain to him that *he* can never be wrong. You have jealousy issues. Addiction issues. Forgiveness issues. You're distracted. You show all the affection of a pet python.

You're actually quite boring.

What he needs to be happy in his life is simple: peace and joy and a bit of affection. Maybe some appreciation. To feel like you need him, that he's contributing and protecting. He doesn't mind the coaching, what he minds is the complete and total disapproval that it feels like. He just wants to be touched now and then, and on all the same levels you used to want it. Most of all, he needs to feel okay about himself, which is not your message lately.

The two of you coexist in a vicious circle. Holding hands all the way down into a domestic hell.

Of course you have your story, and it fortifies your stance. But it might be part of the problem if it remains immovable.

Because of any combination of these parts, he'll go out and find it elsewhere. This guy isn't an asshole, he's just beaten down to the point where he figures he has nothing much to lose. Might as well be an asshole, because nothing else he tries seems to work. The risk-reward math pencils-out for him. He is so without hope or self-worth that he's easy prey for the first painted-on designer dress to glance his way.

Trust me, he knows he's not perfect.

But he also feels—knows—he deserves better.

He knows that this is not a rehearsal, and that the clock is ticking. Just maybe he's the one throwing in the towel before you throw it smack into his face.

Ironic, because from your point of view, other than him needing your coaching and correction, everything in your relationship may seem pretty good. Or at least simply okay. Nobody's perfect, right?

And, of course, you *do* love him.

Right. And that pig flying in your peripheral vision is him, heading for the bar.

This is at once the easiest and the most challenging symptom of impending infidelity to fix. Easy, if you'll cop to your attitudes and commit to a course of awareness and therapy that will result in real change. If you'll just talk to him about what *he* needs. Challenging, if he thinks this is you and you insist he's stuck back there in Reason #10.

Talk to him about what you need, as well, something best conducted in the light of some indication that you're willing to reciprocate. You might be shocked at how anxious he is to make you happy. He thought he'd lost you. He's given up hope for your love affair—that's what he wants it to be, a love *affair*—and your domestic partnership that brackets it. Maybe he's staying for the kids, or maybe he's just afraid of what you might do if he does something drastic.

Like cheating. Sooner or later, that may become an option.

Just don't make the mistake of believing you have all the time in the world to start the ball rolling.

Reason #8: You can't, or won't, give him what he says he needs.

There's such a thing as being dead right, with an emphasis on *dead*.

This one cuts to the chase: he's interested in sex. You... not so much. You prefer "lovemaking," and while he says that's good for him, too, perhaps he defines it differently than you do. Maybe he's interested in certain specific acts, the playing out of fantasies, things that confuse you, possibly disturb you, or just plain don't make sense to you. This happens all the time, way more than even your closest friends will admit to.

Or maybe it's *your* fantasies that are the problem. Maybe they cut too close to those romance novels you no longer admit to reading, and he knows he can never be that steroid guy on the cover. Books he's never read, by the way, so how could he know?

You can't know until you dig beneath the surface.

And so, without that deeper dive, you say no to what he wants, which may actually be what he believes he needs. You ignore it, hoping it will go away. Worse, maybe you judge him for it, belittle him for what he says he wants. You make it sick and wrong. Or just plain funny. Not worthy of being taken seriously. Maybe you and your friends compare notes and have a good laugh about it.

Big mistake. Unless he's Father Theresa, and if he wants it badly enough, odds are he's gonna cheat on you to find it. Even if everything else is going swimmingly. That's how powerful his sexual desire is. You were his first choice, you had your shot, and you said no.

Even if he doesn't seek fulfillment elsewhere, through your judgment and rejection you've rendered him quietly unfulfilled, even miserable. Which breeds resentment. Which inevitably leads to resistance, followed by revenge. Which causes him to lean into Reason #9, which we just covered.

Either way, you lose. Because it's not going to go away.

So now you have a choice to make.

There certainly are things men want that cross the line of tolerance. Women too, by the way, just so you know; in fact, when he cheats on you for this reason and finds what one bestselling female author terms *a simpacato-sickie*, that's the woman with whom it will happen. And she might be just as normal as you are.

But here's the news: that line can and should be defined by the two of you. Together. Without your mother's prudence or fence-line. Without your judgment. With courage and curiosity. With love.

Any counselor, therapist or doctor worth their certificate will encourage bold exploration and the stretching of boundaries. You may be quite alone with your disapproval, perhaps quietly knowing that you are echoing the speculative disapproval of others, like your mother or your friends. Some of whom might be quietly role-playing in ways that would make your mother call her pastor.

Nobody is suggesting you compromise your comfort zone. Just take a look at it, see where it stretches. Again, with love. The real question is, what's the harm? Where does love start and stop? Where does normal begin and end? And who gave you, or him, the right to say, or to judge?

The message here isn't to climb into a wetsuit and a goalie mask and recite the Kama Sutra at the foot of the bed while he laps up grapes from a dog dish, his hands tied to the bedpost with licorice whips. (Unless that's what one of you wants, in which case, head to the store and go for it.)

Not the point. The point is this: there are *consequences* to the choices you make in this realm.

Trust me, there are things you want that defy his understanding, too.

Maybe he wants to stretch the definition of what's okay between you.

Maybe he just wants to jungle f**k once in a while. Regardless of what he wants, rest assured, it's also what he needs. He may not admit to it at that level, but that's the deal. He wouldn't have risked your disapproval if it wasn't.

Or maybe he's waiting—praying— for you to take the first step in making it okay.

The dashing of hope—yours or his—is the most destructive thing in a relationship.

Shut him down—shut his deepest desire down—and you've dashed his hope all over the pillow case. One of the consequences, should you stick to your mother's definition of what is good and proper, is that he just might search out what he needs from another source.

And you'll get to be dead right after all.

Reason #7: The bait worked. The switch didn't.

Things were hot between you, once upon a time. Maybe not a goalie mask and licorice whips, but true, good old fashioned jungle f**king. With a slathering of romance and love to make it all okay. In the car, on desks, swinging from hotel window treatments… it still makes you blush. You freaking wore him out. How could he not fall in love with you?

Good for you. He'll never forget it.

And that's the problem.

Cut to years later, in real life.

He's still a fine specimen, a great guy, kind and generous, and you really do get along, everything considered. But… you just don't need or want sex with him all that much anymore, maybe not at all. At least in *that* way. The only jungle in your life is the backyard that you wish he'd mow more often. You've changed, mellowed like a fine wine. This issue differs from the previous one, wherein he wants a certain thing from you that, perhaps literally, rubs you the wrong way.

No, in this case, you simply don't want his *thing* at all. While he wants what drew him into the game in the first place.

Who he married, sexually speaking, isn't who he's married to now. You expect him to be okay with this. You certainly are. But guess what: he's not okay with it.

He may not mention it, which is another symptom altogether. But that doesn't mitigate the risk that he'll cheat. You might even blame menopause (once again, welcome to being "dead right"), but the sad fact (for both of you) is, he's still testosterone-fueled and horny, and you're not.

You may have forgotten what it was that rang his bell, but rest assured, he hasn't. He wants it again. In the jungle. And just as hot.

Except now, regardless of the rules of reality you've helped write on that line in the sand for the two of you, he has a choice—to accept it and deal with it... or find an outlet for his needs.

Not all men are strong enough, or moral enough, for the former.

Even if everything else is working fine.

Go back to the bait store, kiddo. Because, like it or not, there's more than one fish in the sea. And some of them are wearing wetsuits.

Reason #6: You already left him… for your kids… for your job… or because of your own despair.

He no longer comes first for you.

In his eyes that's a form of adultery, in a way, or at least a form of betrayal or abandonment. If other factors are in play—a tense atmosphere at home, dull or empty sex, a lack of appreciation that makes him feel like part of the furniture—if he's ripe and ready and the kind of guy who goes after what he wants no matter what… then chances are more than remote that he'll cheat on you because of it.

Or at least consider it. Or wish he could consider it. All of which mean you have the same level of problem on your hands.

And when it happens, in a rationalizing sort of way he'll feel justified. Even if another man has nothing at all to do with it—you're too busy for that, too—let's face the truth: he *is* part of the furniture.

At least from your point of view.

Your life is busy and complicated, he needs to deal with that truth. You expect him to be okay with it, because you are. It's your family, after all.

You really do take him for granted, and if he ever dares speak his mind on this issue, you feel like he's doing the same toward you. You've got a life, obligations, other interests (some of which he might actually appreciate and fully support, or so it seems).

You, too, feel justified. Welcome to counseling.

This dynamic applies to other things besides sex.

Hobbies you once shared. Friends you once both enjoyed. How you spent alone time, quiet time, together. Maybe some of that has changed. Maybe he pines for the old days, when you were buddies, co-conspirators, in this together.

Maybe you've moved on to other interests.

Justified or not, at the end of the day there's nothing left for *him*. You've forgotten how to be sexy, at least with him. And if you haven't forgotten what he needs, then you've certainly disregarded it, if not disrespected it. Anything remotely erotic or even romantic has sunk to the bottom of your very lengthy list of priorities.

Soon you will sink to the bottom of his.

Reason #5: Mr. Johnson has left the building.

The opposite situation from #6 can be even worse.

You're a great person. Still pretty, funny, generous, warm. Things are just fine at home. He kisses you hello and goodbye, buys you great presents. But, if you're completely honest, you have to admit that things are a bit chilly in bed these days. St. Paul in January kind of chilly. Not because you don't try. You do try. But lately he's got the libido of a smoked ham, and you don't really know the reason. You can chalk it up to male menopause, you can chalk it up to diluted hormones. Whatever.

The risk is, whatever you chalk it up to, you just might be wrong.

He just doesn't want you like he used to.

And because you're an enlightened woman, you understand that the drives that make a man want a woman are often different from, even in conflict with, the logic of a happy home. Men have needs. So you try to be sexy, come on to him now and then. Speak sweet somethings into his ear. Or not so sweet, if that's his thing. But nothing works. He's dead meat, beyond Viagra, immune to what used to work.

It would be a mistake to write it off as simply a loss of sexual desire. The contrary might be the case. It might be something else entirely that's taken the air out of his hose.

Your job is to find out what it is.

Before he cheats on you. Even if it's only in his chilling heart.

Maybe he doesn't respect you like he used to. He married a strong, ambitious woman, and he found that aspect of you deliciously attractive. He looked up to you, you were a badge of honor for him. But that's not you anymore. You've built a home together, raised his children, supported his career.

Maybe you resent that, and you're not as good at hiding that resentment as you think you are.

Or maybe, perhaps more than likely, have spent years building a career of your own. You've been a partner and friend, and the last time you looked, a pretty good lover.

Whatever it is, it's unfair as hell. That's how you feel, thus adding fuel to the quietly escalating fire.

But remember, he's a man, and men don't think and rationalize like you.

Which means the logic elevator might not reach the top floor on issues with a hint of emotion involved. Especially if hormones are in play.

There are any number of reasons he could lose interest in you, despite your best efforts. Including simple boredom. Maybe you once shared a dream, and it never happened. Maybe it was a dirty little secret—the secret sauce of many relationships—one that has since been white-washed. Maybe he feels unworthy, a failure despite your unflagging support. Maybe you've put on a few pounds (men are shallow that way), and because he has, too, you expect him to go with the flow. You're not kids anymore, so grow up already.

That's the problem. He's *too* grown up and not all that happy about it. He wants to feel young again. To feel alive, to taste it. And chances are, unless he's from Reason #10 or #1 to come, he's too nice a guy or too cowardly to actually tell you what's on his mind.

But not too nice to have a fling with someone else.

May I recommend you look into a chemical option here?

Testosterone therapy worked for me, and has worked for many men to restore not only their libido and a more youthful performance, but to shore up waning feelings of worthiness and flagging energy. Talk to your doctor, this absolutely needs to be a medically-supervised proposition. It might be the secret sauce, literally, that can help restore you to your normal.

The point is to square off with the issue and make some changes. Aging is a process, one that sometimes calls for extreme measures. Like taking the lead in turning your lives upside down, for the purpose of leading back to right-side up.

Reason #4: You think talk is cheap.

Like most meaningful relationship issues, such as emotional fulfillment and conflict resolution, enduring sexual satisfaction between long-term monogamous partners requires work. Regular work. Strategic work. Sometimes guided work. Too often, neither partner understands this, and/or they are ill-equipped or unwilling to do the work. They allow their sex life to atrophy.

Which for men, too often translates to infidelity.

The natural physics of monogamous relationships have built-in governors called boredom and obsolescence. Familiarity not only too often breeds contempt in relationships, it also breeds temptation. If you put your sex-life on autopilot, if you don't work on it, it just might crash and burn.

The scary part of this might be that you'll be totally shocked when he cheats on you, because you had no idea at all that he had needs and desires (which are different and both worthy of respect) that weren't being met.

You never talked about it.

You never asked. He never offered. The issue has become an elephant in your bedroom.

And because this might be just as true for you, he may have noticed and assigned meaning to your apathy. Which, because the two of you don't talk, could lead to disaster.

He won't cheat on you because you don't talk. He'll cheat on you for the other reasons defined here, and those often come to fruition *because* you don't talk.

Do the work. Before someone else wants to talk his ear off.

Reason #3: Then again, it's really about more than just his sexual needs.

At the end of the day, men want what you want from their life partnership: they want to experience meaning.

Okay, they want earth shattering orgasms, too, but roll with me here.

They want to feel strong and attractive. They want to be needed. They want to feel safe and secure. They want to be wanted (yes, sexually, as well as other ways), they want to be taken somewhere with their lover, or by their lover. They want to grow, to evolve, to experience new things, to reach new heights of fulfillment.

Isn't that the same list of things you want, or at least once wanted?

How are you doing with all that? You may be screwing his lights out, but are these needs being serviced, too? For both of you?

Actually, *serviced* is the wrong word.

If you think of his needs as something that must be serviced, nothing more than an obligation—even if you address them happily, in a wetsuit, and even if you have the occasional orgasm while you're at it—if it's all about keeping him fat and happy, if it's not remotely about you in bed, then you can't possibly, at the end of the day, satisfy him to the point where another option never crosses his mind.

He may not know this, but the key to his sexual bliss awaits on the road to your sexual bliss. Waiting for you to work with him to pursue it. There isn't a mature man on the planet who would either reject or look unfavorably upon a woman who is actually asking for something in bed.

Despite evidence to the contrary, men *are* complex.

The old adage "three hots and a cot" may have worked for mom and dad, but those were different times. Today it's a recipe for disaster, not to mention the mindset of a complete moron. You need to give him more credit than that.

Fact is, what he wants more than anything in the world in bed is for you to be hot and horny and creative. As a first option, he wants you to be the woman he's having an affair with. Trust me on this. If he doesn't, you have another problem on your hands, and it requires a shrink or a pair of cardiac paddles.

He may not agree. For him, it may just require another option.

Reason #2: No blood, no foul.

This one is simple. With one dark exception—buckle up, it's next—we've run the gamut of reasons he might cheat on you (other than the possibility that he's into something else, which is another seminar altogether). But none of them, per se, are what sends him out the door.

That decision skates on thin ice. It might be impulsive, an explosion of bad judgment in response to a specific incident that triggers something within him. It might be the result of a growing attraction taking place outside of your field of vision (read: he's being a shit at work, engaged in or on the cusp of an affair of the heart). It might be a well-planned betrayal. It might be an on-line liaison gone too far. It might be someone with an eye on him, and the flesh is weak.

Whatever. He's human, after all. As are you.

One factor applies to all of these, and you have almost complete control over it: the likelihood that he'll get caught. The higher that probability, the less likely he'll cross the line. The fact that he wants to is another issue altogether, and it's something you should pay attention to.

Get in front of the problem.

One way to make him think twice about taking his equipment on the road is to make sure he understands the consequences. Many women succeed here by defining a "one strike" rule—he won't get a second chance, and the fuse his cheating ignites will explode his world. Show him the phone number of your lawyer on your Contacts page.

If his urge is a casual thing, a shallow restlessness or curiosity, he might just set it aside when he compares the benefits to the significant downside. He'll think of it as an investment, a risk-reward proposition, and your job is to make the risks significantly motivating. As in, terrifying, but without a gun held to his head. Hint at vicious lawyers who will take him to the proverbial cleaners. Evoke images of reciprocal whore mongering, the loss of this children, even that middle of the night bat to the bridge of his nose, which is actually more common than you'd imagine.

Whatever it takes. Make sure he understands the stakes. Because for a man on the verge, fear works much better than guilt. Just be careful how you handle this type of leverage, because it can come back at you.

It can't feel too much like a threat, even though that's precisely what it is. Don't give him something to defy or resent. The more subtle, the better. And, the scarier. Cling to your justified rationale at all costs. Don't seem too eager to exact this revenge before the fact, as if the very thought of it is already gratifying.

Another strategy is to make it hard for him to sneak around.

This one is risky (not to mention the fact that it will piss off civil libertarians everywhere) because it puts you in a position of appearing to lack trust, or be nosy or controlling, which, in a Shakespearean twist of irony, might become the very thing that pushes him away. Your risk isn't in being branded with those labels, the real risk is in being wrong. It may be a risk worth taking, because that's precisely what you want to be in this instance—wrong.

So be it, you may have reasons to feel paranoid. Make a habit of dropping in on him when he least expects it, when he's out with his "buddies," at the bar or the golf course where he's supposed to be, even at work. Learn how to monitor his computer activities. Smell his clothing when he comes home. See if the shirt in his gym bag is moist, and if it feels more like tap water than the product of an elliptical trainer. Make sure you get a peek at his credit card statements and phone bill. His mobile phone also has a nifty little feature that allows you to see who he's called, and who's called him. If he guards it like a precious stone, pay close attention, something may be up. If he deletes all this data on a regular basis, step up the intensity and frequency of your nosiness.

Let him see you doing all these things.

Mostly, trust your instincts.

When it comes to cheating—unless you're the insanely jealous and insecure type—they're rarely wrong. And if they are, consistently, then look in the mirror, where another story is playing out.

If he's good at this slimeball stuff, you may need to resort to more drastic measures. Short of installing electronic surveillance, a private detective isn't as ridiculous as it sounds. Nor are they all that expensive. But consider this first: if things are that bad, and that obvious, it's probably just a matter of time before he steps in it.

Reason #1: His moral compass couldn't find North if it had a picture of Santa on it.

Welcome to the worst case scenario. At least, back at Reason #10, you're still in the conversation, loud as it may be. You began your journey together based on flawed criteria. You may or may not have been able to adapt. That's what #10 was all about.

With this one, you're history. You always were.

One word: *snake*.

Once in a while it all comes down to this: the guy simply can't honor his vows of monogamy, whether spoken, written or implied. Even within what seems to be a wonderful marriage or partnership.

Bottom line: he's a schmuck, and there's nothing you can do about it. Sooner or later he'll cheat on you, regardless of your efforts or empathy. It's inevitable, even if you're perfect. He can't not cheat—because he's weak, he's selfish, and/or he's stupid. Plain and simple, when all is said and done, you're living with a scumbag.

He won't see it this way. He'll say "it's complicated." A phase he's going through. A momentary weakness. Something you brought about. Cut him some slack, he's just a man, after all, and men have needs. And he'll pull out all that verbal joie de vivre that hooked you in the first place to convince you to give him another chance.

Complicated, it is. For both of you.

Sadly, this snake scenario happens all the time.

Chances are you know someone who has lived this nightmare.

It happens perhaps even more than the other reasons cited here. The others imply some measure of hope, they have remedies, there are conversations to be had, pain to be relieved. Often those remedies work, the underlying causes are treated before an adulterous transgression comes to pass.

But with this guy, the snake… get in line. There are support groups waiting for you. You may think you know who you're married to, but that may not be the case.

By the way, there's plenty of two-by-fours at Home Depot. I'm just sayin'.

The bottom line.

If you've noticed a common thread here (and if you haven't, consider the possibility that you're in denial), it's this: each of these symptoms and states-of-mind drive men to the point at which they face a choice: to cheat on you, or not. Like a good doctor who addresses the underlying causes of impending disease, you need to go deep into your relationship, into him, and into yourself. When you're there, pay close attention to the details.

How close is he to that decision point? How close are you to noticing?

What are the things about your relationship that create distance between you—world view, religion, politics, habits, family stuff, money, health issues—that might lead to a dark string of frustration or resentment or hopelessness, which are the precursors to cheating?

Relationship health, like physical health, is not a given.

It's not even a right. You have to maintain the body of your relationship. You have to feed it well, exercise it, be good to it. Even dress it up from time to time, take it out on the town. Even then, doing all the right things, bad things can happen. There are natural laws, human forces in play. You have to diagnose symptoms and apply the right medicine.

Across the vast landscape of relationships in this country, the most frightening truth of all is that too few couples realize this, or have the courage or willingness to do anything with it, or about it. They're on autopilot. They don't give a rip anymore, because the mountain seems too high. Or they simply aren't looking up to see it. They can't handle the truth. They're stuck in a descending circle that is nothing short of vicious, wherein they're willing to give only as good as they get. Where resentment and old programming rule the household.

The result of that, among other possibilities, just might be infidelity.

If you don't want him to cheat, do everything in your power to take the choice away from him. That's all you can do. You can't make that choice for him. But you can position the choice, give it consequences, push it to your side of the fence, offer him better options right there at home. The extent to which *you* change, provide what he needs, *becomes* what he needs. And in doing so, it is imperative that you clarify what you need, your willingness to join him on a journey of reinvention, of healing and the cultivation of hope.

I'm not suggesting that you compromise, either what you need or where your line is. Quite the contrary. I'm suggesting that you say it loud and proud, that you stick to it, and that you sell it to him as the path to peace, and eventually to bliss.

Inherent in that, of course, is the fine print... that you'll do some listening and, if required, changing, as well.

The degree to which you embrace these options is the extent to which you can truly say, at the end of the day, that you did all you could do.

Healing your relationship is always a complex negotiation that takes place on two fronts: between the two of you, and within yourself.

You, too, have a choice, and on both fronts.

Part Two

A Wake-Up Call*
For Men

(*Things women wish their guy better understood.)

Ten Reasons She's Going To Leave You

At the beginning of Part 1, the wake up call for women, we considered this:

> *Men leave women for another woman.*
>
> *Women leave men for another life.*

For too many guys, this means she's gonna leave you flat. Maybe without warning. Or at least that might be what you'll think. For some guys, they have absolutely no idea what those two sentences even mean.

So let's do this like men. Straight at it, straight up truth.

She'll leave because life with you is, among a long list of specific grievances, as frustrating as it is less-than-advertised, as dull as it is hopeless. It takes a while to get to that point, but the journey is downhill, and it's a slippery slope.

If what was once a raging fire is now a pile of unattended ashes without a trace of its former warmth, if that Prince Charming costume is more than a little snug around the middle these days, if the center of your universe is a cold brew and a flat screen from Costco, if the only reason you don't "get it" that she's bored silly is because you haven't thought to look her way between anniversaries, and worst of all, if your behavioral bullshit—let's call it what it is—is bigger than the macho denial you cling to like your dear mother's breast (because real men don't talk about feelings after all) then start shopping for an apartment and a cheap ride.

Since most real men wouldn't recognize a romantic metaphor if it crawled up their ass, consider this: time always cools the passion of new love. But if nothing other than a jointly-filed 1040 and a few Hallmark cards remains between you, if you have temper problems and insecurity issues and unhealthy addictions, consider those warning signs. If her family makes your skin crawl and you rationalize golf as exercise (it's not; you burn more calories masturbating than you do riding 18 holes in a golf cart), not to mention a scary menu of other deal killers, sooner or later your relationship is going to be at risk.

Tough talk? The truth often feels like that.

When the day arrives that she admits to herself that life is too short, and if she spends it with you it'll seem all too long, she'll be history.

She's gonna leave you, dude.

Unless you get your shit together.

And if she doesn't, she just might dedicate the rest of her days to making your life miserable.

In the vast majority of cases, here's what it boils down to: it was *your* fault. Your relationship went on autopilot, and you're the pilot caught napping in the cockpit. Sure, it takes two to sink to new lows, but by and large, at the end of the day it was probably you who became emotionally delusional. Either because you didn't know—the eternal dying plea of men on the verge of being alone—or you didn't have the balls to step up to the plate and change.

Men are quite willing to change, by the way, but it's usually after the fat lady has sung... to her lawyer. Most of her contributions to the shit-storm will be issues of self-preservation, rage, lack of clarity (pain does that to a woman), and perhaps even revenge (it does that, too).

Not to mention the venomous advice from friends who have been there.

What you think is her contribution to your troubled times is, if you look more closely, likely her reaction to your decisions and behaviors, and it just might very well be just as toxic as your contribution to the shit-list. But that's not the point. If you didn't give her something to get pissed about, none of this would strike you as nauseatingly familiar.

This is not to say that things weren't once grand and passionate.

They probably were, once upon a time. But shit happens in the standard contract between cohabitating lovers. Bad shit. Things change, life's little pressures pile on and time marches forward, with or without you keeping in step. These are the physics of love and marriage. The fine print of that contract, which neither men nor women think to review on a regular basis, says that to survive you must change with those times, navigate the fickle winds of maturity and grow with her instead of watching her sail off into the sunset in pursuit of a new dream... without you.

Understanding the fine print of relationship maintenance is a beautiful thing. It is also quite rare. Which is why half of all marriages fail (Google it), and why much of the other half wallows in mediocrity and apathy. We forget that relationships require work.

Autopilot is so much easier. Trouble is, autopiloting your relationship will, sooner or later, send it cartwheeling down the runway.

Life is too short.

It's time to cowboy-up and do something about it. Before she lawyers-up and does it first.

In a nutshell, there are things you are doing, right now—you may or may not be aware of them—that are eroding the foundation of your primary relationship. Little drops of acid that will, over time, burn a hole in the door through which she'll walk. Every time you do one of these things you take another chip out of the trunk of the tree of your life together. (That voice you hear, the one that smacks of non-stop complaining, is your wife yelling "timber!" at the top of her lungs.)

The two-fold bad news here is that these behaviors have become habit, and you have become deaf to that voice.

She may be no more capable of confrontation or even recognizing these issues than you, or she makes the mistake of silently tolerating and then resenting you (good luck with that one), or perhaps neither of you can spell *i-n-t-i-m-a-c-y* without averting eye contact or breaking into a cold sweat.

You may have no awareness—you probably don't—that these are things she thinks about. Bad on her, but it doesn't change a thing relative to the outcome, or the root causes. Women aren't always perfect, and it's entirely possible, though not likely, that it just might be her fault as much as yours. The difference is that if you are truly the victim, you probably won't leave (men don't have the stomach for it), you'll just sink further into your cocoon, surrounded and comforted by a cushion of silence, to perpetuate an endless circle of pain.

And/or, you'll have an affair. Then you'll get caught, and it will be your fault after all.

You see, shit does happen. But that's another counseling session. You're not getting out of this by citing quid pro quo.

What follows here are ten of the most common, and most deadly, of relationship deal killers from the men-are-pigs point of view. Not saying that men are pigs, as a generalization, but there are enough of them in the herd to give us all a bad name.

The goal is to not be *that* guy.

The good news is—at least where nine of the ten pigs are concerned—their effects can be softened or, if you're willing to let go of your inner linebacker, they can be eliminated from your playbook entirely. Scars notwithstanding, the damage can even be reversed. Not that it will be easy—each one merits an entire shelf at Barnes & Noble.

The first step in this journey is recognition, followed closely by the courage to be vulnerable.

What happens then is the hard stuff, wherein you and your significant other must face the music and head down a road that will test you to the core. That's called open and honest communication, and chances are you suck at that, too, or you wouldn't be in this mess.

In a word: counseling.

One more thing. Don't be seduced by the notion that most of these Neanderthal behaviors don't apply to you. They probably don't. But know this: any one of these chinks in your husbandly armor can get you a condo on singles row. Any two, and you're advised to learn how to do laundry all by yourself. And if three or more of these sad states are in play, it's only a matter of time until you're watching *The Playboy Channel* at midnight by yourself. At least—and this is the ironic part—if she has an ounce of self-respect. (Most women do, they are amazing creatures; if she doesn't, you have a whole different set of problems).

Buckle up. This isn't going to be pretty.

Reason #10: You equate sex with orgasms.

Which is another way of saying—and this is not meant to be remotely literal—you suck in bed.

Over the years the act has adopted the choreographed precision of a pole vault. You prefer the lights off. No, you demand that the lights be off. You bury your face into the nape of her neck at the moment of truth (yours... hers rarely crosses your mind). The bedroom—the only place sex happens for you—is as quiet as an embalming suite, save for a few opportune grunts (also yours). The one time she suggested something new or kinky—and trust me, it'll only happen once—you shut her down with a healthy dollop of ridicule.

Maybe—and this really happens, much more than you'd think, I know of two relationships where this is/was the case (neither of them mine)—she's never seen you naked.

In short, when it comes to things sexual, you have more stockpiled bullshit than a fertilizer factory. You don't have the slightest notion what makes your woman purr. Hey, you've been doing it this way since college, it worked then (when all parties involved were clueless or drunk, or both), why change now?

Not you? Let's see.

Here's a little test. Be honest.

What would your level of comfort be if, at the moment of your orgasm, your wife (or life partner, whatever) took your face firmly in her hands so you couldn't look away, gazed piercingly into your eyes and insisted that you stay with her, that you not look away as you come—as in, have an orgasm—to lock eyes through those entire few ecstatic moments as if to consume your pleasure for her own.

As if that moment of eye contact was part of the orgasm itself.

If you shudder at the thought of such intimacy, and/or if you can't picture your wife going there, welcome to couples counseling. Chances are neither of you are all that creative in bed. Or at the very least, you're letting the best in life pass you by.

Once again: it's spelled i-n-t-i-m-a-c-y.

The solution is as simple as it is frightening and foreign to most men. It's a secret that some women don't even understand, but everything that falls under the heading of "sexual healing," not to mention sexual bliss, is related to this fundamental truth:

The most sensitive sexual organ in a woman's body, without exception, is her mind.

This is a gold nugget of truth that can change your whole life.

One that opens all sorts of terrifying doors for men with intimacy issues. It means eye contact. It means real communication, understanding what your lover wants and then giving it to her in ways and means she has never dreamed of. It means using words, even nasty little stories, as eligible playthings in bed. Lighting, music, scent, location, dress, a flat screen, vegetables, all are borne on the pallet of the enlightened lover. Who knows what she's thinking about when you're not in the room.

And it's all perfectly fine. It calls for you to do something different, to take a risk, be creative, to *think*, to be proactive. To be focused on her (which wasn't how you did it in college).

Let me free the cat from the bag and cut to the end game of this issue: If you can truly say this is true for you, as well...

... that *your* most sensitive sexual organ is, in fact, *your* mind...

...then you have one foot in the winner's circle. Because such men are rare, and they are treasured. Trust me, this is precisely what your partner wants. That is, if their libido has even a breath of life left in it.

But then, how could you know any of this?

That would require talking about it. It would demand intimacy, it would call for the courage to go where no man—at least you—has gone before. Deep into her mind.

If you don't go there soon, someone else just might.

Not buying this?

Here's another little test: just ask her.

I dare you. If she doesn't sign on, then chances are you share an intimacy issue, and the chances of ever embracing bliss together rank right up there with winning the next Powerball. That, or she's already given up on you. Which means the odds are gone altogether.

One final observation, and it's a monster. It sets the stage for sexual healing and the positive growth of your relationship. It is the precursor to bliss. Here it is: myth holds that men and women are from different planets when it comes to romance and sex.

It's just not true.

For many it's true to some extent (that extent being rooted in dysfunction), though even for them it's a socially-inspired convention, reinforced through generation-linked gender roles that allow them to hide from true intimacy.

The myth would have us believe that women, as a universal truth, want to "make love," to be held, to be whisked to a place far away in their imagination, a place where Danielle Steele and that ripped guy on the cover of a romance novel dwell.

To connect, to touch souls.

The same myth says that men just want to get off. Whatever it takes. Hey, if it gets you laid, you'll give it a go. The only thing you want to touch is her ass.

But consider this: in virtually every conversation you'll have with women who are frustrated with their man's skills in the sack, you'll find a yearning for the exact opposite. Sometimes they just want, if you'll pardon the term, to *jungle f**k*. To be wild and wicked. To be desired, to be taken as an inevitable consequence of that desire. To drive you over the edge with such desire, to take *you*.

And/or to be taken in ways you'd never imagine could occupy a cell in her innocent little brain.

Sometimes she just wants to get off.

But even if that's what she wants, at the core of that need is the hope that her partner—you, or whoever, because soon it may not be you—will have at least some awareness of her presence north of her navel.

That you can, indeed, spell intimacy.

Irony is, the worse you are in bed, the more they want something wild. Women want passion. They crave excitement. To feel like a woman again.

Which is precisely why she just might cheat on you someday. Or worse, leave you flat.

She wants and needs some sense—her unique sense—of romance and love, if not the trappings. If you don't deliver, someone else might.

What men often don't get, though—and this is terrific news—is that she still may want to screw her brains out, every bit as much as she wants it to look like a love scene from a Jane Austin novel.

It's a foreign concept to most men. Sex without intimacy, over time, translates to failure. Which again is ironic, because she'll leave you just to get back to that jungle where the passion resides. To feel alive again.

Be warned, Tarzan lives in that jungle. He's out there.

It's complicated.

Then again, it's not.

If you're completely honest with yourself, if you have the courage to go deep and confront your inner clueless son-of-your-father self, you may find a surprise: that you, too, are a simple yet complicated mass of seeming contradiction. Because while you do indeed want to get off, you also want to be loved, to be held, even to be taken.

Thus, the same basic sexual truth applies to the penis-handicapped of the species, whether they are man enough to admit it or not: the most sensitive sexual organ in the human body, men *and* women, is always the mind. Proof positive: picture Margo Robbie naked at the foot of your bed, or wearing something you'd prefer to her nakedness… that's something that can only exist in your mind.

Meeting in the middle, where romance and passion melt together in a white-hot heat of love-making, you just might discover your mate again. The lover you thought was long gone. This is where you'll reconnect, or perhaps discover, a shared dirty little secret.

This is the secret weapon of love, and it's available to you.

This is where and how you'll find your bliss.

Be assured, bliss of the sexual variety will take you a long, long way down the road toward a larger, more meaningful peace and happiness together in all aspect of your lives. At any age.

Don't expect her to take you there. It's a dance, and women like to be led. Or at least asked.

If all this gets you thinking, then there's hope for you. If you have no idea what any of this means, know this: she does.

And you're already in deep shit.

Reason #9: You are tone deaf to the music of your co-existence.

Context—the nature of the energy between you—is everything in a relationship. And it's not just true about sex. It's even truer when it comes to co-existence with your life partner. Your lover. The person with whom you live and to whom you've promised the best version of yourself.

Are you delivering on that, day in and day out, twenty-four seven? That's the goal. Impossible to meet, critical to strive for.

How are you doing on that front?

A DLS (Dirty Little sex Secret) goes a long way toward creating a sense of intimacy, and it's a buffer that can help weather the not-so-sexual challenges (like you coming home drunk), which are inevitable. But the context needs more than erotic tschotskis and fantasy scenarios to make the partnership work over the long haul.

We've all been with couples who radiate all the warmth of a chilled smoked salmon appetizer. They are constantly sniping at each other, cloaking it with a biting wit. It's a sparring match between standup comedians with an agenda. They don't touch. At first they may actually come off as entertaining, fun to be around. After a while, though, you feel sorry for them. You admit that you're glad you're not them. Sometimes, usually fueled with alcohol and surfacing backstories, their banter gets out of hand and you have a public spectacle on your hands. Eyes avert. Nobody laughs, except the victim/orator.

If you are that couple, odds are you'll defend it as harmless. A schtick, just having a little fun. But be careful not to project your skewed view of reality onto your partner, even if she gives as good as she gets. Just because she can stay with you on the court doesn't mean she enjoys the game. It might only mean she's as witty and mean and vengeful as you are when cornered. That she understands the concept of survival. It may mean that she knows the best defense is a good offense. Could mean she's simply trying to save face in front of her friends. And that deep inside, she'd like to rip yours right off.

Not a good thing to let fester for too long.

Here's another test, the acidic kind, to assess the *tone* of your relationship.

Imagine you and your wife are just beginning your relationship. That she is, in fact, still dating other men, and you are competing for her hand. You're in love, but for her the jury is still out. You're on trial, you're being tested and evaluated. If you can accept that premise, now be honest about how you are with her—spoken and unspoken—at home, in public, alone, with others. How you are with her in moments of stress or distraction. What is the temperature of the water in which you swim together? Would your way of relating, your tone and the energy it creates, win you the girl in such a scenario? Are you someone she'd honestly say is fun to be with, is kind, considerate, someone that has her interests at the top of his list of priorities? Are you still her Prince Charming, her Marlboro Man?

Didn't think so. That's not reality, you say. After a while that would be silly, you say, it would feel contrived. It's just not you. Real life just doesn't work that way. Nobody acts that way after a while.

If that's your response to failing this test, then welcome to the holding pattern of love. Welcome to autopilot. Because if warmth and consideration is *not* your reality, if you think it's silly and contrived, if that's just not you—even if the tone of your daily life is otherwise without any real negative sentiment at all, it's just sterile—then ask yourself this: why would this woman, a woman who knows in her heart that she deserves to be happy, give anything better in return?

What price is being paid over the long term? And, are you willing to pay it?

One answer is scary as hell: you're leaving the door open—indeed, you're plopping out a welcome mat—for someone that will treat her better, someone who will make her feel beautiful and appreciated and loved on a daily basis.

This is where the oldest cliché of marriage counseling becomes valid: enduring love and the happiness it brings requires work. Hard, confusing, sometimes unrequited and unappreciated work. The effort, the toughness, the selflessness, and the warmth it creates, must happen every day. Even if it's only coming from you. If you engage in a joust of defensiveness and coldness, someone will get knocked off their horse.

And if you are waiting to get before you give, that horse will drop a load on your head.

Okay, so you're not the most romantic Joe on the planet.

She knew that about you going in, and she'd smell a fake rat the instant you brought home a $4.99 bunch of flowers from Albertsons. Fine. Nobody is saying you have to be Enrique Eglesias. Fact is, though, that the concept of "romance" has as much to do with the day-to-day tone of your relationship as it does with foreplay. And to some extent, every woman wants romance, or at least appreciates the effort, however the two of you define it.

Do you still kiss hello and goodbye? Hold hands in the car, at the movies, walking through the mall? Do you compliment her without prompting? Call her during the day just to hear her voice? Do you indulge in random acts of kindness and gentleness? Do you still flirt with her? Brag about her right in front of her? Do you anticipate her needs, and then exceed them? Does she catch you just staring at her for no reason other than the fact that you can't tear your eyes away?

It doesn't matter that she rarely directs any of this behavior back at you. Like some things, this one isn't a quid pro quo proposition.

The odds are high she doesn't—like it or not, romance has always been a bit of a one-way street—but if you can begin to incorporate this into your daily behavior, she'll find a way to return the warmth in her own fashion. Every day that passes in which you don't show her that you love her by doing these things, by injecting even the most subtle hint of romance into your time together, you are a day closer to the end.

If not the end of your relationship, then to the hope it will grow into something fulfilling, something that resembles fulfillment and bliss.

Every woman wants to feel loved. To feel special and beautiful. To be wanted.

Skeptical? You know couples that don't seem all that romantic or warm, and from where you sit they're doing just fine. He does his thing, she does hers, they show up and have fun, they don't argue, it's all just hunky-dory on the surface.

In fact, you may think you're doing fine, too—like them, you don't admit how empty you feel to anyone—without all this contrived affection and gazing and open communications crap that makes you squirm.

Here's the dark side of that: those people may have settled. They've given up hope. The "work" they do in their relationship is to maintain the status quo, to avoid icebergs. They do what they have to do to get by, to maintain the façade of tranquility. They hold it in, and for a while it seems to work.

They've given up.

Fine for them. Fine for you, too, if that's all you want.

But unless you energize the tone between you with warmth, whatever that means for the two of you (what works for some indeed may not work for everyone), you stand little chance at complete fulfillment.

Because like antioxidants in the body, like money in the bank, like a strong and chip-free trunk of a tree, a healthy and warm foundational tone in your relationship is the buffer you'll need when conflict happens, when that iceberg pops up on the horizon.

Which they inevitably, always do.

One more thing about tone, and how it sets the stage for everything else, from sex to peace and quiet to happy vacations to iceberg-wrangling and a future you actually look forward to: in this day and age, women rarely settle over the long term.

Our mothers, maybe, but times have changed.

In this century, if mama's not happy, at the end of the day she'll either leave you, or make it her life's work to make your existence as miserable as hers.

Reason #8: Your conflict resolution skills suck.

Like a pitcher with a wild streak, a golfer who can't putt, a singer with stage fright, or a politician with an eye for the ladies... this one will bring you down. Even if you're a great provider and companion, the best lover since John Mayer. The funniest fellow in every room you're in. Or the consummate coach and cheerleader. If you can't help but turn into a flaming, incompetent, self-destructive dick when the two of you don't agree, sooner or later you'll be on your partner's shit list.

Ladies, this one applies to you, as well.

There are lots of pitfalls in this arena. Your temper is hair thin, and it gets the best of your better judgment when it takes over, prompting you to draw blood with your words and—here it is again—your *tone*.

Then you wake up and feel like the shit you are. You beg for forgiveness (which she gives, and then hates herself for it and, every time it happens, resents you more for it). Maybe you don't fight fair—you dredge up old issues, resurrect resentments, slap her with guilt trips, withdraw, and/or generally intimidate her in any way possible.

Or, you triangulate—a technique that cornered people use to bring an irrelevant issue to the discussion. Example: she's pissed at you for embarrassing her in front of friends, and you come back with the fact that her friends are all social climbers anyway. This diverts her intended focus on your own perceived guilt.

Maybe you just lie your way out of trouble.

Or—and this is a common one—you can never be wrong. If that's you, and you're married to a woman who also can never be wrong, just call a counselor now. Or a lawyer.

As bad as these in-the-moment grave diggers are, though, these after-the-fact poisons are just as acidic: you punish her with the silent treatment, especially when she's in the wrong. Sometimes it lasts for days. Or, when it was you who messed up, you pout. You hold a very palpable grudge. You file it away for the next confrontation. You make her feel guilty for being right, because it made you feel lousy when you weren't. Worse, you find ways to get even in subtle and insidious little ways—you withhold affection, you withdraw, you sabotage.

They don't call it the war between the sexes for nothing.

At the risk of misogynistic cliché, women are famous for clamming up when conflict hits. They don't want to talk about it. They want you to just go away, which (and they may not realize this, but it's worse if they do) is their way of letting you know how angry they are, or how much you've hurt them. But men do it, too. If you're the type that needs to get it over with right away, then (bend over) it becomes their way of punishing you. You contribute to the long-term effects by letting them get away with it. Or by joining her in this nasty little game of brinksmanship. It's a game in which everybody eventually loses.

The best we can do here is ask for your awareness of how you behave when the heat is on, and then challenge you to be bigger, to play at a higher level, to not need to be right, to win or to punish. Rather, you're willing to consider a future-you in which you are open and vulnerable. A partner who sees her side of things. And admits when he's an ass. The goal is to love her, unconditionally, during those times of conflict. To give her the ties. To allow her to hold you accountable, and have the courage to do the same for her, without punishment or guilt.

That's what this is all about: a future you.

In essence, the goal is to be Dr. Phil, but with abs.

More likely—you need a referee. Our response to conflict—men and women—is rooted deep inside our psychology, and our psychology is usually bigger than we are. A good first step is to pick a time when you're not fighting and—OMG, here's that communications thing again—ask for honest feedback. Ask if the way you handle conflict makes things better or worse for her, if it's remotely effective. If she feels loved. Be ready to shoot the same feedback back at her. Try to agree on the rules of conflict, and to put it in perspective.

A little tip: bring a full set of catcher's gear to the conversation.

Know this: if you're an abusive fighter, you may win the battle while losing the war. She might leave you one day, right or wrong.

And if she doesn't leave you right away, her new life goal will be to make you miserable before she does.

Reason #7: It's all about you.

Newsflash: a woman's place is not in the home, and her purpose in life isn't to make you happy and comfortable. It may be her choice to live this way, but if you think of it as anything other than that, you're in risky territory. In fact, you're in schmuck territory.

If you really want it to work, it needs to be all about *her*.

Times have changed, and more women have changed with it than the legions of men who cling to the notion that their parents had it right. Their idea of gender roles and expectations in marriage may be sorely out of tune with your wife's reality.

While the economics of the day demand that many couples send both halves into the workplace, some households run just fine when one works outside the home and the other takes care of domestic business. As long as all parties agree—really agree—on who does what, things have a chance of working out just fine.

But there are pitfalls along this slippery slope, and they usually involve a husband with his head parked well behind his sphincter and a wife who recognizes a double standard when she sees one. It goes back to a law of marital physics, and when it comes to domestic and economic roles within the partnership, things don't usually remain fat and happy for long. At least in the mind and heart of the woman who gets the short end of the deal.

Let me reiterate… this issue is defined by the truth of what the work-at-home domestic manager feels about it. If she or he is happy with this, if this is her dream come true and her passion, then this discussion becomes one of appreciation and empowerment, with anything close to taking it for granted becoming the toxic component.

Often things start out with this seemingly mutual agreement. And often, things go quietly sour with its terms.

If you both work, yet it's her role to feed you and continue to care for the house at the end of the day, unless you handle it in a manner that defies all probability, sooner or later she'll resent you for it. Especially if she senses, even for a moment, that you take it for granted. Or if you view her work as less important to the family than yours. (Feel free to reverse the genders of this). If your idea of a great Christmas present for your partner is a new blender for your drinks, you better grab a clue before she or he grabs a tire iron.

If you don't know where the Brillo pads are, you're in for trouble.

This is as true for mothers as it is for empty nesters. Scary.

If you have a career and your partner remains at home, and you consider weekends your well-earned time to golf or fish while your better half attends to the kids' games and an assortment of domestic chores, sooner or later she'll resent you for it. Or worse, she'll thank the heavens that you're out of the house. Either way, you're on the road to ruin.

If you get to retire someday, and she/he doesn't because, hey, "women's work is never done,"… that's trouble in Reality City.

If you go anywhere near the belief that your work is more important than her work—especially if her work is caring for your children—even if you're a brain surgeon and she irons your lab coat, she'll resent you for it. And then she'll find a way to punish you for it.

If you give her the third degree over the grocery budget and make her feel like a criminal for buying yet another pair of shoes you don't think she requires ("why do you need shoes when you never go anywhere?"), and yet you don't hesitate to grab that new fly rod when it goes on sale, sooner or later she'll resent you for it. More likely she'll quietly hate you for it.

Welcome to the line for the window at which you make another deposit into the account full of things she must forgive you for, because it's already on the list of things she resents you for.

If you prefer watching the news during dinner instead of engaging in conversation, or if the notion of helping to clear the table and do a few dishes is as foreign as watching *Dancing With The Stars* with her (even though it's her favorite show), sooner or later she'll resent you for it.

If you laugh at her desire to get a job after the kids go off to school (my wife lived this one in a prior life... hence, why she's my wife now), if you don't talk politics or investments with her because you don't think she'll understand, if you choose your vacation based on where the fish are hitting or where the Superbowl will be played or the proximity of a new casino you just read about, if you insist on the last word regarding wall coverings and furniture placement and other issues of the interior decorating you've already delegated to her, if you have rules about when and where you eat out and/or on what nights certain cuisine must be served at home, if it never enters your head to ask her about her day when you get home from yours, if the only time you tell her she looks nice is if she asks... she'll inevitably and absolutely resent the hell out of you for it.

Scarier still, she may not breath a word about how she feels. Or more accurately, how you make her feel.

Even the most angelic of partners in this scenario will find insidious little ways to punish you, in ways you will never be able to assign blame.

Do any of this long enough, and she'll leave you. If not literally, then emotionally.

And that, my friend, is what hell on earth is like.

Reason #6: Your dark side trumps your many charms.

From all outward appearances, nice guys lose good women all the time. Sad but true. One of the reasons is that they may have dark secrets—not the dirty little kind shared by lovers—that surface too often and too big in the relationship. Secrets that spring from the pile of un-recognized psychological bullshit connected to their past, or worse, from a lack of character.

Of everything on our list of reasons she might leave you—or, is going to leave you if you exhibit too many, too often—your dark side can be the deadliest. Some of these traits have and will surface elsewhere in this survey of relationship deal killers, but take heed, they can be either a contributing factor *or* a deal breaker on their own.

If you have an addiction problem—alcohol, drugs, pornography, tobacco, gambling, sports, whatever—and you refuse to listen to her pleas to get over it, sooner or later she'll stop empathizing and tolerating and she'll start resenting. And that lights a fuse which you may not be able to snuff.

She just might leave you because of things that, from her point of view, you love more than her: your addictions. And when that moment arrives, it may be something else entirely that snapped the chain, leaving the poor whimpering guy—that would be you—without a clue about how he really was the corrosive agent that weakened the chain in the first place.

If you have a temper problem, if you blow sky high at the slightest provocation, even if you have a legitimate case when your top blows, you are doing irreversible damage every time it happens. It becomes *abuse*. It's a huge chip out of a fragile tree trunk. Verbal abuse can get you single as quickly as physical abuse. And with abuse of any kind comes a loss of a sense of safety, which every woman since Eve has absolutely required, as a minimum benchmark, to be happy.

When they're not happy, they leave.

One way or the other. They can leave you cold, or they can remain with you... cold.

Speaking of physical abuse and the loss of safety... if you hit her, even if you just shove her around now and then, you deserve to lose her. And you will.

Get help. If you do it even once, she'll never forget it, even if she claims she's forgiven you. Chances are she's lying, or simply mouthing the words.

If you do it again, you've validated the suspicion that you're an abusive ass, and once she summons enough self-esteem and outside advice, she'll leave you flat. Even if it takes a restraining order. She might even plant a two-by-four between your eyes in the middle of the night. Whatever it is, you can count on major consequences coming your way.

Then, of course, there's the infamous green monster.

This one is bigger than you are, which means you need professional help if this is the issue that's driving both of you crazy. Her past bothers you (hint: get over it). You resent that she admires Ryan Gosling's butt (to your friends, you say things like, "hey, the guy isn't all that hot, right?" Guess what: he's way hotter than you). You tell her you suspect she flirts, perhaps that she's messing around.

Jealously doesn't work. When you turn green, you're killing off the love.

This next one is insidious, because everyone goes there to some extent, hopefully in a minor and rare way.

That said, now know this: your repeated casual relationship with the truth can get you a casual relationship with a divorce lawyer. Bending the truth to make yourself look good, to hide things you'd rather she not know (such as a little slush fund, a lunch with an old girlfriend, some time on your favorite porn site, etc.), especially when it occurs over time and thus becomes part of your personality, is a betrayal of trust. And as you'll read in a moment, that one can be a knife in the heart of your prospects for a happy future with her.

If you defend this because of fear of some unreasonable reaction on her part—be honest on this one, it's usually fear of her being right—then you have another issue that requires attention and clear, courageous communication.

The Big Kahuna of reasons she'll leave you.

There is another addiction that kills a relationship faster than a death certificate, and while obvious, it bears discussion: cheating.

Actually, it's entirely possible to survive getting caught with another woman. Not likely, but if your woman is somewhat of a saint, and if the rest of your behavior warrants keeping you around, and if you pay enough sincere penance, you just might get a reprieve. Don't kid yourself, though, things will never be the same between you (are you ready to pay *that* price?), but you might get to keep your side of the bed.

Don't test these waters casually.

Because like lying, and to some extent all of these dark behaviors (especially abuse), it isn't the act of cheating itself that will send her sprinting out the door. It's the damage it causes, the resultant loss of trust and respect. Some toothpaste just can't be stuffed back into the tube.

Once trust, safety and hope are gone, so is she. If not physically, then certainly in her heart.

Reason #5: You... the dream that never came true.

There is a secret ingredient in the pursuit of domestic happiness. It's not sex, it's not money, it's even not peace of mind. Those are by-products of your time together, and they're more like basic elements than secret ingredients, ligaments held fast in part by your avoidance of the behavioral traps described here.

All that aside, know that there is one single thing that can forgive all sins and keep the relationship moving forward, and that you play a huge role in it.

It's called *hope*.

The hope that you, as a couple, can solve your problems (read: she's praying that you can rise above your bullshit). The hope that you will experience the things you once talked about. Maybe you were going to save the world. Maybe you were going to climb mountains together. Find God together. Start a company. Retire in the sun. Help your kids live a better life than yours.

It is the hope for growth, both intellectual and emotional. The hope for health and well-being. The hope that you'll love each other more, and enjoy your time together more, as you grow old together.

The hope for bliss.

For her, you once represented that hope.

Ask yourself this: how are you doing on that front today?

Ask it as you lie on the couch watching yet another football game. Ask it late in the afternoon after you've been golfing or fishing all day, every Saturday, while she does something else that's not quite as much fun. Ask it while she takes off to a family function you've managed to weasel out of. Ask it when the choices you've made for your career and your finances cause her to forfeit something she holds dear, even if it was just a wish. Ask it the next time she fakes an orgasm, or worse, doesn't bother.

Ask it the next time it seems you don't have much to say to each other.

I'm not saying that you don't have a right to your hobbies, to some time for yourself, some "guy time" if that's your thing. Indeed, you better find a way to carve some out, or you'll have a whole different set of problems.

But ask yourself this: how is the dream coming along?

Granted, it's tough enough to cover the basics. To be a good provider and a good lover, to be kind and occasionally romantic, to be her best friend over the years, to live honestly and with healthy choices, to bottle up your bullshit and manage it, because she's worth it.

If there's a pit in your stomach right about now, caused by the question of whether she's really worth it, stop everything and call a counselor, because you're smack in the middle of a vicious circle that is bigger than either of you.

Nothing easy about it, for sure.

Then, once you've wrapped your head around this one, along comes yet another challenge: to in effect be on guard for seemingly insignificant behavior that, over time, can blend too much vanilla into your life. That might bore her, give her the wrong impression about you. Behavior that allows her to lose respect for you because, perhaps, you've lost it for yourself.

The next step after that is the loss of her hope.

The nice thing about dreams, and the hope that fuels them, is that they can usually be resurrected. The smart man, the man in love, goes into the resurrection business. Gets a Ph.D. in hope resurrection.

Every day he wakes up next to a woman he loves, with a full appreciation of it.

While the dumb guy, the guy with DGS (Dumb Guy Syndrome) eventually gets dumped.

Reason #4: Once best friends, now roommates.

This is a tricky one.

Because not all women are created equal. Some women will work with you, tolerate you, until things settle into a rhythm they can live with. There is usually some measure of reward in it for them, even some bliss (maybe their expectations weren't all that high), but they don't seem to be trying to move forward all that quickly, and they certainly aren't trying to change you or your relationship.

Maybe they're just happy to be there.

If that's your domestic situation, odds are you can survive living with her (or him) as your best friend. If that's enough for her, and if it's enough for you, happy trails.

Some women, however, want more.

They want growth. They want passion and excitement. Challenge and reward. They want to laugh and cry with you. They want you to remain on the pedestal upon which they once imagined you.

They still want it all.

How are you doing on that front?

You might be a perfectly nice fellow, void of most or all of the relationship cancers described in gory detail here, and it still might not be enough.

The key is right here, in each section of this little user's manual.

Take a look and ask yourself not just how you're doing, but how can you take it to the next level. Then ask her that very question. The goal is to be very clear about what she wants and needs.

And—get ready for it—to, with a pure heart, subordinate what you need to the passionate pursuit of it.

The goal is to become the giver in the relationship. To outgive her, every day.

Because if your lady is one of those dreamers, even if you're eligible for husband of the year... if you're no longer her dream come true, however she defines it, right or wrong, she just might leave you someday.

Reason #3: She no longer trusts you.

The phrase—"he just doesn't get it"—is one of the most commonly uttered clichés on the planet among newly single women, and unhappy women who are disappointed.

In the end, it all boils down to a stew with five ingredients: trust, respect, safety, hope and joy.

The net flavor, the result, is called *love*.

Maybe not award-winning, Dr. Phil, George and Amal kind of love, complete with movie sex and great fortune, but love nonetheless.

You see, theoretically she loved you when she moved in. From there it can go in one of two directions: it can grow, or it can deteriorate. To not grow is, in fact, to deteriorate. The quality of that five-ingredient stew is the determinant of the direction. No trust, no safety, no respect, no hope, no joy (sex is a sub-set of that, by the way)… no love.

Simple.

You may be wondering where intimacy went, why I haven't included it in this list. Reason: intimacy is the result of, the consequence of, the simmering of these five ingredients over time.

Chew on that… intimacy isn't an act, it is a *state*.

The ironic point isn't as much about what you do, it's about how it affects the woman in your life.

Here's an absolutely terrifying newsflash for you: you have zero control over how it affects her. None. Out of your hands. The only thing you have control over—and this is the ironic part—is what you do. How you are with her. The effort you make.

The consequences can and should be predictable, but unfortunately that's not always the case. Hence, this list of behavioral caution signs.

At the risk of oversimplifying what thousands of years of history tell us is anything but simple, these are the fundamentals of keeping her around: trust, safety, respect, hope and joy. Each one is a chapter title, within which there are countless definitions and options.

Like Tina Turner asked, what's love got to do with it?

It, too, is a consequence. Love is a word to describe how you feel. And while we talk about "an act of love," that is too often confused with a good deed, when in fact, love is the product of how you *are*.

Love was a beginning point. From there it evolves into a consequence of the combination of those five key and precious relationship ingredients. Which, again, are trust, safety, respect, hope and joy.

Love is why you offer trust, safety, respect, hope and joy.

And thus, love is the fuel of domestic happiness. Bliss is merely a degree of the state of love you feel.

If you want more than simple coexistence, you have to take it to a higher level.

The behaviors that erode trust, safety, respect, hope and joy are deal killers. The behaviors that enhance the outcomes of those states of being are the most powerful tools in your bag for attaining bliss.

And if bliss is her ultimate dream, pay attention. The bar is high.

Reason #2: She no longer respects you.

Your behaviors have consequences, and if the consequences of your temper, your addictions, your petty jealousy, any physical abuse, cheating, lying or otherwise threatening her trust, her safety, and the dim prospect of joy, you can add one more deal killer to the list: the loss of her respect for you.

When that happens, you're doomed.

Respect isn't critical for a relationship to survive.

It is critical, however, for it to *thrive*.

If bliss is her goal (and it probably is, at least if she still clings to hope), and if you stand in the way because she can no longer respect you, chances are she'll begin to think about living another life. One with a shot at the big dream.

Scary stuff. But it gets worse. There are other, seemingly innocent little traps into which you can fall in this regard. Small stuff. Temporary stuff. But they are toxic, and over time they can wear her down. Accumulate enough of them, next to some of the larger deal killer behaviors, and they become that thin little straw that breaks the poor camel's back yet again.

Here's a few: you think football is life. You think spending every Saturday playing golf and then cards and then coming home half in the bag is your birthright. You feel your penis entitles you these pleasures. You say your chemical attractions aren't important in the real scheme of things. You believe there is woman's work and there is man's work. Her friends are just that, her friends. "Guys night out" is a God-given privilege. The louder the better. Outside of work you have the depth, meaning and complexity of a crossword puzzle.

None of this is wrong, per se. You're entitled to an opinion, and to your alone time and your guy time.

What it is, when taken to extremes, is stupid. Because these are things that can erode what once was her sense of respect for you. These are the things you will regret when she pulls the plug.

Reason #1: The phenomenon of *snap*.

You've heard of cause and effect. Pretty much everything I've covered until now has been in the category of cause.

This one, the #1 reason she'll leave you, boils down to the inevitable effect of all of those once seemingly harmless, normal, toxic autopilot behaviors and habits so common to marriage and primary relationships.

Sooner or later, she's gonna snap.

And once the snap happens, you're gone.

If you don't stop the bleeding by fixing these toxic relationship wounds, the day will come when she does, in fact, snap. She's had enough, and the point of no return will have been crossed.

Every woman who has ever left a man for these reasons snapped before she hit the door. Or more likely, showed him the door.

Bottom line: when things deteriorate to this point, to the point of snapping, she already realizes she wants another *life*.

One without you in it.

You've tossed one too many bales of hay onto that poor camel's back. The specific incident that put her over the top may not seem all that egregious, but that's not the point. She's quietly tolerated you for years, maybe for decades, maybe until the kids are gone, maybe until someone she trusts gives her the courage to make a move. Maybe she snapped a while ago, and she's been biding her time (and talking to her lawyer). Like water over a rock, years of erosion may have worn her down (or toughened her up, depending on one's point of view). Because of this, when the shit-storm hits, you'll cry foul all the way to the bar. And then to your day in court.

But she's done. Once and for all, and irrevocably. Game over.

The scary thing about women is that when they snap, nothing you can do or say will make it okay. Sure, you might talk her into coming back, but the echo and resultant scar of the snap will overwhelm the good intentions of a second chance, which you never really had. The snap fuels her intention with strength and righteousness. It's bigger and stronger than you are.

Yes, second chances are granted all the time.

But that doesn't mean the game isn't over. It means she wants to be sure it's over.

Sometimes, in retrospect, a woman fears her snap was more of a warning test-snap that she couldn't differentiate from the real thing.

But real or faux, irreversible damage has been done. When the second snap comes, and it usually does, it happens much more quickly and irrevocably than the first faux one you've talked her into rethinking.

Unless, of course, the man actually changes his ways.

But even then, it's usually too late.

The good news is that women usually give their men plenty of notice that a snap is on the horizon. Years and years of notice, in some cases. From there, if you happen to perceive the danger at hand, it's completely up to you.

Carve that one into your forehead: it's completely up to you.

Few of us heed that warning, if we even notice it.

If we do acknowledge her cry for help, even try to make amends, too often this simply signals a period of temporary calm (which she needs as much as you), about which we make up a story that says everything is all right. A bouquet of flowers, a few empty promises, then after a few months its status quo, back to the ballgame, the one we were already losing.

The good thing about men is that we will get it, but it usually dawns on us when we're alone sprawled across a used couch in a rented apartment watching the high definition LED flat screen she never wanted anyway, wondering what went wrong with our lives.

It was you all along. All too often, beneath and behind everything you can validly explain as her fault (*her* bullshit, if you prefer), there was you.

There is no remedy for The Snap.

Like a fatal disease, hope resides only in preventative measures and early detection.

Simplicity on the other side of complexity.

It could be argued that it's all pretty simple, and from one point of view, it is.

Treat her well. Love her well. Make her feel beautiful and special. Lose the bullshit. Try to make her dreams come true (trying is much more critical than accomplishment itself). Hold each other accountable to high standards. Talk to her. Be interested in her. Grow together.

Be a man she can love and respect.

Don't cross lines beyond which there is no return. Don't be boring and don't be an asshole. Simple stuff.

How to get there, however, how to manage the myriad challenges of living with another human being... these aren't simple at all.

There are givers and there are takers (nearly every relationship assigns those roles, even though it may be difficult to admit), and those roles can and must be managed. Accountability is required from both sides of that casting call. Doesn't matter who is who in that equation, the taker isn't necessary the bad guy. There are partners with issues, partners with pasts, partners with situations and excuses.

It can all work, if you want it badly enough. If you communicate.

And, if you leave every negative behavior you've read about here in the locker room.

Otherwise, the odds are good that, in spite of what can be argued is simple, someday she'll snap. She'll simply leave you flat. If not literally, then emotionally.

Man to man.

One more thing. You may be somewhat pissed off right now. Perhaps discouraged. Even righteously indignant.

That's natural, you've just had your entire relationship paradigm shoved past your sphincter. One response, the good one, is to sit her down and own it. To commit to your growth as a partnership, through your growth as a man. Only then can you ask for her end of the improvement equation—undoubtedly you have grievances, too.

All of this can be gender flipped, role flipped, turned inside out. Because all of this can apply to all of us. It's critical that this message resonates. You may not be the bad guy. Then again, you might be.

More likely, it's both of you, in complex and insidious ways.

Another response to this information—and this is the kind of thing that got you in this jam in the first place—is to say *screw it, I have a right to be who I am, everybody knows I'm a great guy.*

Except, perhaps, her. When the one person who knows the most about you doesn't buy into your own perception, that's something to look at.

I am who I am is a confession, not a defense.

I'll never change is the battle cry of the defeated.

I'm a proud man is the exclamation of the already lost.

Every person who hears you say that will immediately understand why your marriage or primary relationship tanked. Why you are now alone, back on the market, perhaps having learned nothing.

So go right ahead, stick to your father's guns. Sneak around back and have that smoke she resents you having. Go ahead, go fishing this weekend, again, while she runs the kids to their games. Go ahead, clam up, be the man your daddy showed you how to be. Show her how strong you are, by showing her how lame and stubborn you are.

But do it at your own peril, my friend. Because she's watching, she's feeling, and the clock is always ticking. She gets to choose how to respond to her feelings.

Now it's your turn to choose.

One last analogy.

Think of your domestic problems as a pit you've fallen into, one that you dug, handful by handful, each time you've been guilty of one or more of these transgressions. Think of it as a well, a wishing well—you wish you could take it all back, make her happy again, have a great and blissful relationship.

You wish you weren't so self-interested and clueless. She wishes that, too.

Now think of her love for you, her willingness to work with you toward making it all better, as a rope, one she's tossed down to you many times, one that she's constantly unraveling, cutting you slack.

Here's the deal with that rope: each time you are cold and moody, each time your temper flairs, each time you are clueless in bed, each time your behavioral bullshit surfaces and your double standards do double time, each time you cross the line and beg for forgiveness... each time, the rope gets shorter.

What's lost from the rope will never return.

If there's enough rope, hope remains. Unless you keep digging yourself deeper into the hole. If that's the case, you're getting burned on both ends of the analogy—her rope is shrinking, when it needs to get longer to reach you as you descend into the ever-deepening pit of your own husbandly ineptitude.

Someday that rope will no longer reach you.

There'll be nothing to grab onto. Where before she'd toss it down and, with hopeful tears still in her eyes, help haul you out of your hole—with a fervent prayer that you won't take a running full gainer back into it—now you are completely on your own in that dark place that is the bottom of the hole you've dug for yourself, with no rope and no hope that can reach you.

When the real snap goes down, she won't believe you, and she won't forgive you. No slack remains. You must try to resurrect a flat-lined relationship. Picture her standing at the edge of the pit, gazing down on you as you try to claw your way up and out.

What's that expression on her face?

Pure evil. At least, that's what will it will feel like in that moment.

After all the times she's tossed down her emotional rope and, with all her strength, pulled you back close to her, now her face is void of humanity. Her eyes are dry. She might even have a dark little smile that is more sad than wicked.

Because she knows. She's done. She's sad because it didn't have to be this way. The smile is because she can now begin to find that new life she's been longing for. She's on the cusp of cutting a cord that she now knows should have been severed before this.

If any of these symptoms describe you, then the snap is immanent.

A false snap, the test-snap, is like a trigger that's been pulled, and only nanoseconds remain before the pin strikes the bullet that will blow you away. You have precious little time left. If you do nothing, the false snap quickly gives way to the real thing. But if you can make it out of the hole before she steps away from the precipice altogether, leaving you down there to die—the metaphoric equivalent of cutting off any chance of saving your relationship—you'd better be a different man than the one she's been living with.

And trust me, when you do… she still won't believe you.

You better become the guy she thought she married back when—the guy in the dream—or if she was clueless, too (which she might have been, only she got a clue over the years, while you didn't), more like the man she needs today.

Grab the rope now, wrap it around you and bring her closer than she's ever been. Hold her there, even though she'll squirm at first, try to get away. That's her pain trying to protect her from the false starts you've shown in the past.

Your odds are low. But they're all you have.

It's time to man-up.

Because just as the pit is one of your own digging, if there's any rope at all left for you—after you've summoned the strength to climb out—then you really can fill that dark hole up again, day by day, one handful of your discarded bullshit at a time.

Part Three

THE DOMESTIC WARRIOR'S TOOL* CHEST

(*awareness, not drill bits)

Five Case Studies in the Blame Game

Here is a little perspective on men, offered to women who are frustrated with us.

If you've read this far, you're getting the gist: men are very often the pigs we are rumored to be by their cynical, worn-out mates. Or at least too often dumb as a box of Twinkies when it comes to primary relationships. Because of this, this section is aimed at women narratively—I address you directly—with an agenda of speaking to men just as clearly.

Because it's good for both readers to understand it's not always our—the man's—fault. Even when it starts out that way. Sometimes the response is worse than the transgression.

Most men actually do try. We get it right often enough, but the contrary is a fair assessment just as often as not. I'm not about to defend or even try to explain our infuriating masculine ways—for that I recommend a hefty psych textbook and a semester at a quality grad school.

This chapter is about surviving those awkward little behavioral moments that so frequently occur in our company, regardless of who crossed the line first. Because even though your guy might make Howard Stern look positively suave, you just might be making things worse with your oh-so-justifiable responses.

There are many more examples than these, of course. My hope, though, is that the context of these situations ring familiar, and that you might apply a keener awareness to any of them the next time a weak moment strikes.

Every one of these real-life situations—irritation, frustration, surprise, bad choices, mean spirited humor, accidental ineptitude… the stuff of living together—is an opportunity to be a better version of yourself, to exemplify the commitment you've hopefully made toward creating bliss in the life of your partner. And in doing so, for yourself.

Usually, though, this is where sparks fly.

Words wound, old tapes emerge. Recovery is slow. Resentment is in the air, it becomes a cloud that must dissipate. Sometimes that process takes too long, fostering an atmosphere of discomfort and fear.

Because I am one (a man, that is, one who is constantly working to conquer his inner swine), I know from where I speak. So allow me to do so for the entirety of my gender as I acknowledge something you already know: it's pretty much all our fault. At least with the big picture stuff.

But those moments—the lesser responses to those moments—are equal opportunity offenders. Women speak with sharp, wounding tongues every bit as often, and as consequentially, as do men.

This, my wife will testify, is something I know.

We men are natural wallowers in the muck of relationships.

We are too often clueless, completely and utterly, and while we love you desperately—and some cases, like my own, I mean that quite literally—we continue to occasionally behave like the animals or children we are, depending on your metaphoric preference. We drive you bananas with our inexplicable appetites and affections and blind spots, our impatience, our lack of taste in interior decor, not to mention our eternally frustrating inability to read your always organized mind, irrespective of the convoluted words that might spring from it. (If you accept that any of these generalizations are valid for men, then please at least accept that on occasion those of your gender spill out words that seem not to have a relationship with each other).

That said, this isn't about assigning blame.

Rather, it's about avoiding those subtle little relationship land mines that can blow up without regard to gender or fault, and manifest in an unexpected instant. Step on one, and your relationship takes a hit. Step on too many and you just might lose a leg.

And thus, a paradox: you want to call him on his shit, put your foot down (or insert it elsewhere), or simply express how you feel, and do it without him suddenly pleading to the heavens that he's being attacked. Again. You want him to change, you want him to *hear* you. Over time, your frustration with your penile-handicapped partner may build to the point where you are actually the instigator of trouble, rather than an innocent bystander who gets hit by the debris.

For all your good intentions, you may actually be stirring it up.

And thus the battle becomes a two-way street.

You don't have to swallow our crap to minimize its stench. If you can begin to understand how your response—justified or otherwise—affects him and the big picture, then you might be able to make a better choice the next time he makes you crazy.

Or not. Let's get real, sometimes you just need to let him have it.

Two quick caveats.

First—and you may not agree or even want to hear this—the road to happiness is indeed a hazardous two-way street, and the pitfalls reside in both lanes. As infuriating as he sometimes is, it takes two to triangulate, much less tango. So let's stop pointing fingers, for now at least, and address half the problem: *you*.

There are a few things you may be doing, defensible or not, that send a chill up the spine of your relationship. You may not be aware of them because, believe it or not, he might just be swallowing as fast as you are.

And second, there are bigger mountains than these to climb in the geography of relationship rescue. Mount McKinley kind of bigger. Chances are most of these issues are tips of deeper icebergs (hence my use of the term *iceberg-wrangling* earlier), some of which require more than your enlightened response.

But until you get serious about fixing things on that level, here are five trying and depressingly common situations to look at in the meantime, mirror in hand, and make the best of the next time he squeals like a pig.

1. You don't recognize that guy behind the wheel. And you don't like him, either.

Let's start small. He's driving, you're watching. Coping, perhaps. Someone cuts him off, he swears like a character in a Melissa McCarthy movie. The light changes, the car in front of you doesn't move quickly enough to suit him and he labels the driver with a body part that rhymes with *bass pole*.

Never mind he had a bad day at work, maybe he looked at his 401K balance before you left home. Regardless, suddenly he's your father, or the old boyfriend you dumped for this very reason, and it pisses you off.

This happens several more times before you get to the multiplex, and you find yourself defending the targets of his verbal assaults, suggesting that perhaps they had a bad day at work, too, and that the bass pole in this situation might just be him. You find yourself suggesting ways in which he might alter his own driving habits, and before you know it he's giving you the silent treatment (by the way, what he's thinking about you in that silent moment is the landmine), or worse, the exact opposite.

Sure, he deserves the best you can dish, but now there's trouble afoot, and the evening just might be ruined.

What's wrong with this picture:

To go straight at it... you're kicking him while he's down.

Sure, he's acting like the king of all bass poles, but despite the indefensible nature of that truth, it's not the point. He's doing it because something is wrong in his world. It may be you, it may not be, but you can be sure, when you heap more pressure and disapproval on him by jumping his case about the way he's acting, it *becomes* about you. He feels unsupported, misunderstood, unjustly attacked, and in that moment, unloved.

Right or wrong—and we both know it's wrong—he'll resent you for your righteous commentary, and that resentment will manifest itself in some dark way, either through an argument-commencing comeback, or later on with his own carefully-crafted criticism. A skewed and triangulated response, to be sure, but do you really expect him to be rational mere seconds after he's flipped off a van carrying a girl's soccer team?

Hopefully later, when he's more rational, he'll bring it up and you can have a productive discussion about what happened, and your response to it.

A better approach:

Sit on your response and talk to him about it later (don't wait for him to initiate)—and do it calmly, opening with an apology for jumping him—when he's more open to your feelings. Follow the apology with a statement like, "Honey, when you (*insert bass pole behavior here*), you make me feel like (*insert righteous indignation here*). Remind him that you know he's bigger and better than that moment of weakness—go ahead, lie—and ask what's been eating him to cause him to regress to Cro-Magnon Guy.

Act like you really care about his answer (if you don't, refer to the aforementioned icebergs). If that won't work, then at least watch your tone when you intervene in his little traffic tantrum. And if all else fails, suggest—calmly—that he let you drive while he tongues a pacifier in the back seat.

2. Oh *that?* It's just his little "thing."

He pulls the car to the side of the road to watch an airliner on final approach. Every time, like he's twelve years old. A Corvette passes by, and to your great horror he tells you yet again he's always wanted one of those. He puts ketchup on his steak. He watches music videos in bed and always has to make a comment about Beyonce's backside. He leaves the sports section on the floor next to the commode. He orders the same thing at The Olive Garden, every single time. There's an old shirt in his closet that looks like it should be wrapped around a broken pipe, but he wears it every weekend. Golf is his religion of choice, Scotch on the 19th hole his sacrament. Maybe there's a frilly little ditty—perhaps not so frilly, perhaps even inexplicable, but a ditty nonetheless—that you know he'd really like you to wear to bed, even though you've shamed him into not mentioning it anymore.

He does these things year after year, ad nauseum, until it makes you want to hire a hitman. Nothing you say has or ever will change any of this. So you've given up.

Well, not quite—now you just roll your eyes, toss out a clever diss, maybe embarrass him if someone else is around, share a group giggle at his expense. In your darker moods you make sure he knows you think he and his fascinations are ridiculous. In your lighter moods, whenever these little appetites pop up, you do the same thing, only with an unconvincing smile.

What's wrong with this picture:

While his attractions and fascinations may be harmless, rest assured that your disapproval of them (and especially your intolerance) is not. We're not talking about the hard core addictions here—pornography, substance abuse, unreasonable attraction to other women, steak knives in the bedroom—which remain a legitimate cause for your serious concern.

No, we're talking seemingly innocent quirks and tastes, however far beyond your comprehension they might be. It's the enduring repetition of them that drives you nuts, more than the content. I'm not suggesting that you begrudgingly give him his space; I'm suggesting you should not stink it up with your disapproval.

Because after a period of experiencing your cynical reaction to the things he likes or even loves, in his male mind you are disapproving of *him*. You are creating distance between you.

You've just crossed over the threshold of the papa bear's cave, and you're welcome here as long as you don't pee on his favorite bed of leaves. He doesn't waltz into your cave and start dissing the wall coverings.

Space is almost always a tool that will serve you.

A better approach:

Truth is, he wants your approval. That's why he brings it up... time after time, every time.

He may say he doesn't *need* it, but that's just self-preservation kicking in. He'll settle for your quiet tolerance, but he'd rather share these fascinations with you than not. If you can't quite climb into his head and say, "gee, I never knew—I actually like it in here," then do your best to fake it by keeping that give-me-a-break look off your face when he clicks into geek or perv mode.

The view when you look down your nose is domestically distorted—perhaps not for you, but certainly for him. He'll assign meaning to your disapproval that transcends the harmlessness you might good-heartedly intend.

3. Seize the weekend. Yours, not his.

You love your projects. You start them all the time, the bigger the better. And because your projects are often related to the house or yard, to beautifying or at least cleaning up your life, you have a reasonable expectation that your partner will share your enthusiasm.

You probably wouldn't ask him to finish painting the sky after you've painted the floral arrangement. No, this is about asking for his participation in a way that robs him of whatever he was intending to do otherwise. Things he thought were your projects, not his.

But here's what too often happens—you bite off more than you can chew. Time runs out, it's too heavy, something more interesting comes up. So you call for help: you summon him from the TV or his office or the putting green, whatever, and ask him to finish painting the wall where you can't reach, load the piles of dead shrubs to the dump, to hold the picture against the wall while you move back (and then, using tone because he should know, you inform him he's standing in the way), to plant those eight rose bushes on the side of the house.

Reasonable requests, all. But you sense he isn't into it (what's up with that shaking head, and why is he gnashing his teeth?) Which means that you begin to assign meaning to his resistance, or at least his resentment, something along the lines of him not appreciating your efforts to create a beautiful home, taking you for granted, or worse.

What's wrong with this picture:

You've made the decision for both of you that what you're doing in that moment, perhaps for the rest of the afternoon, is more important than what he has planned. And it may very well be. But it makes no difference if you're right about this or not—most certainly, you will believe that you are—the damage will have been done.

The key factor here is frequency. Depending on his patience and demeanor, you have an account of such favors (that will be his perception of them) to draw upon. But sooner or later that account runs dry and you're overdrawn, invading his precious free time, subordinating his plans to yours. He'll resent it, and not far down that road he'll resent *you* for it.

A better approach:

This one's easy, it gets you the help you need, and it works every time: plan ahead.

Ask—nicely—for his participation so he can put it on his calendar. Or if it's impromptu, be flexible about the timing and, most of all, allow your appreciation—rather than this being his duty—to shine through.

The worst thing you can do is spring it on him.

And by all means, don't judge however he'd otherwise be spending his time as somehow inferior to your agenda, thereby justifying your intrusion. Ask ahead of time and he'll be happy to help.

But know this: in his mind he's not helping you, he's rescuing you, and being the rescuer isn't a bad thing for a man (or a woman, for that matter). Don't, however, resort to this tactic too often—thick as he is, he'll catch on.

4. Communicate, don't triangulate.

You've hit a pothole along the road less traveled and it's time to talk. He has feedback for you, and if you've been paying attention then you know you should let him say his peace, consider it carefully and respond with empathy.

Straight out of the book, right?

Except he's accusing you of not listening to him when he's the world's biggest stone-deaf, zoned-out bad-listener on the planet. He's suggesting that you spend too much money, when he just blew a thousand bucks on a new graphite composite driver and he hasn't golfed in two years. He complains he wants more sex, when the last six times you came on to him he suggested that you wait until Sportsline is over.

Oh, you hear him alright, but when it comes to that empathetic response, you draw the line because it's just so ludicrously unfair.

Instead, you enthusiastically point out his faults and shortcomings on the issue at hand, firing it off before he can finish his own side of the story.

Or worse, on a different issue, such as: he says you've been cranky lately, to which you respond that he hasn't cleaned up his closet in a year.

That gets both of you exactly nowhere, other than irritated.

What's wrong with this picture:

It's called *triangulation*, and it'll snuff out any hope you have of conflict resolution. You're confirming his suspicion that the '80's song by The Spin Doctors called *"Little Miss Can't-Be-Wrong"* was written about you. (Note: mentioning in such a moment that Carly Simon's *"You're So Vain"* was written about him is a great example of triangulation.) Even if you're guilty as charged, he's guiltier of even graver charges, and in the name of all that's just and fair you damn sure intend to make that clear.

But consider this: if you can't be wrong, then neither can he, and you know *that's* not accurate. You also know where this is headed.

Welcome to counseling.

A better approach:

This is one of those situations where you have to haul out the big guns to solve the problem. The big gun here, perhaps the most powerful tool in the mending and growth of relationships, is *vulnerability*.

You may be tempted to triangulate right now as you read this.

Here's the ticket to success: you go first. Be vulnerable, even if he won't. Afterwards, in the glow of your reconciliation, point out to him that it was your decision to be vulnerable and open, and that this made a difference in this silly little confrontation, which he'll undoubtedly believe he won. Which is fine, he needs a win to stay in the game.

5. The best defense is a good, well, defense.

This one cuts both ways. You both do it, and you both suffer consequences from doing so. It's the subtlest and arguably the most critical element of your daily relationship—*tone*.

Tone of voice, tone of facial expression and body language, the ambient tone of the moment. It's snappiness, sarcasm, a palpable lack of affection, an inappropriate response. Its visual judgment and condemnation. It's the venom in your voice and the poison on the tip of the point you are driving into his skull.

On the responding end, it's making assumptions about the darker of implications of something one of you says, assigning meaning based on your own fear and resentment. Sometimes it's offered up as revenge, an exchange of blows, giving as good as you get.

And that's the lighter side, when the guilty party really didn't mean anything by it, it was just an unfortunate choice of words or nuance. A weak moment.

Far more challenging is when what you perceive to be negative energy is deliberate and real, every bit as mean spirited as you fear. But being victimized by tone doesn't change the dynamic, because it's your *response* to these little barbs, warranted or not, that's at issue here. You can make or break the moment with your choice of response, either going toe to toe or simply letting it pass. The former is certainly easier than the latter, but there's a price to pay by engaging.

What's wrong with this picture:

When tone rears its nasty head, it's always a lose-lose situation. If you respond in kind, commencing a baseline rally of barbs, the moment very quickly becomes about the tone itself rather than the underlying issue. If you let it slide, there's a feeling that he's getting away with something, that he's disrespecting you or simply being an ass.

Barbs hurt, so we reflexively strike back. It's that reflex that will get you. Those little sounds you hear are the splinters of the foundation of your relationship cracking and falling away.

A better approach:

Don't respond to tone with more tone on your part.

There's a slim chance your perception was off, or that his approach was a total failure. Ask for clarification—did he mean to sound so judgmental or harsh? When he's shocked you would think that, immediately check your reflexive anger at the door and say something nice. (By the way, he might be lying here; seeing your reaction, he might not want to engage, he was hoping to slip one in—you get to decide if you make the moment into a thing or a lapse in judgment for which you can forgive him). If you're too pissed to talk, then just smile.

Because now the risk has changed—it's you who has become the barb thrower, when indeed his first volley was unintended. So make a different choice. Recognize these pissy little moments and manage them with your head, not your reflexes.

We'll go deeper into tone a bit later, because it's that important, and that risky if you don't understand the risks.

The menu of domestic risk and reward.

There are as many other seemingly insignificant but potentially deadly little relationship cancers lurking out there as there are possible combinations of personalities. Consider the possible permutations.

There are controlling partners who micromanage every decision. There are insecure partners who inexplicably keep their partners apart from their extended families and the things they love, and who play "poor me" games that nobody wins. Sometimes the "dirty little secret" between you is a bona fide character flaw that he pleads to keep to yourself. There are partners who force their values and their world view on the other. There are game players, conflict avoiders, victims, predators, liars, cheaters, cowards, narcissists and the downright sociopathic. There are double standards, triple standards, a total lack of standards, boredom, incompatibility issues, spiritual bankruptcy, selfishness, the patently inconsiderate, arrogance, intolerance, laziness, judgment and, dare we say, piggishness.

Welcome to co-habitation.

Any single one of these creates a context within which you respond and interact. The number of alternatives and choices available are staggering.

What they have in common is that, left unchecked over time, they—and here is where we change to first person and cop to the truth—*we* create resentment, and resentment is the greatest relationship cancer of them all (as opposed to, say, adultery, which is more a relationship bullet to the head). In each case there is something wrong with the picture, there is something to look at and to understand.

Victim or not, you do have the power to make it better. With a little love and forgiveness and a lot of effort and vulnerability—the great relationship healers—anything is possible.

And with an understanding of the realms of relationship that become the emotional landscape upon which it all plays out, your odds of reaching bliss increase by orders of magnitude.

Which is precisely what we'll examine next.

Realms of Relationship

In earlier drafts of this book I wrote about eight pages of introductory material for this section, defining and positioning these realms in a context of rendering them relevant. My wife, who is a ruthless editor, told me it was all too long and redundant.

Of course I knew that, but like any writer we put things onto paper for reasons that make sense at the time, and those eight pages made sense.

In my defense of how I'd handled this—writers always have a defense of their first draft—I said this to her: "Relationships are complex. Much like clouds, drifting and changing shape. How do you describe a cloud to the extent that someone can see the grand plan within? I'm trying to break that cloud down into component elements, so that we can focus in these microcosms and see what is working and what isn't."

She smiled at me and said, "Say *that*."

My wife is whip-smart. I've learned to listen to her. So here is the second of the two pages introduction that remain.

We are all imperfect and uneven human beings. By partnering with another human being, we have 2x the risk of ripples in what should be the otherwise smooth waters of our days. Turbulence is inevitable, but getting away with poor choices isn't. Success isn't as much driven by compatibility and chemistry as it is by the odds of emerging from these confrontations unscathed.

Whether you are in a new relationship with massive capacity for patience and tolerance, or you are deep into a worn-thin, end-of-your-rope endurance test, all of us could benefit from a set of empowering tools that will help us through.

These realms of relationship are precisely that. They create a path toward a deeper happiness by smoothing the road itself. There are five relational realms that are omnipresent in all relationships. Then, there are two in which they may be best applied. And finally, one catch-all everyday realm of dealing with an unending stream of situations, challenges, differences and opportunities.

Being aware of them is the tool. Improving the nature of our understanding and responses within them is the opportunity.

1. The Realm of Safety

In 1943, a psychologist named Abraham Maslow published a paper in the *Psychological Review* entitled, "A Theory of Human Motivation." It changed everything we thought we knew about what made us tick as functional, relational beings, while triggering an evolution of management strategies in business and governance, as well as offering a richer basis for understanding what makes personal relationships work, as well.

It begins with what we need at the most basic level of our existence. And once we have that, what we need next. And then again, after that. And so on.

Take a look at Maslow's pyramid, which shows our most basic need at the bottom (our physical well-being, the need to stay healthy, fed and properly housed), on up to what happens when more fundamental needs have been met. The highest level is a state of self-actualization, something few of us ever completely attain. It covers a breadth of states, not just one's job or one's domestic harmony. This is, perhaps, what motivates a billionaire who seems to have everything to run for President—he/she is seeking some form of self-actualization, beyond the esteem, or the illusion of it, they have already attained.

As we work our way toward that state, we pass through other layers of need. From there things get more complex as we pivot the focus from survival to our place in the world.

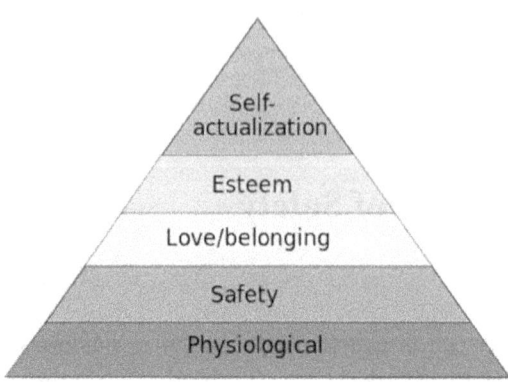

Notice the second most basic need, right there above the realm of our physical necessities: safety. It's even more basic than our need to be loved. Which could lead to an illuminating conclusion: for love to work, we must first feel safe within its embrace.

A cynical person might add, "Sure, okay, as long as you feed me first." And while I offer that in jest, there are indeed some people who will rationalize themselves as an exception to any theory or advice, and then resent the hell out of anyone who tries to tell them otherwise.

If you're married to *that* person, you may be even more challenged to find common ground in these principles.

Consider the realm of safety within primary relationships.

So many other words come to mind as ingredients in the whole of our safety in this arena—the freedom to speak our mind, to speak the truth, to act as we choose, the consequences of crossing certain lines. And in some cases, a risk of violence that is either physical or emotional, or both.

But the notion of safety becomes a consideration long before any risk of violence applies. Because there are so many ways to make a mistake, either getting hurt or hurting someone else in the process.

If you are afraid to speak up because you fear your partner will bite your head off—because that's what they do, they snap at you—or to say what you need or how you really feel, then you are dwelling in the darker corner realm of safety. Because you don't have it to the degree required to safely speak up or take action.

Allow me to share from my own marriage to illustrate.

I've confessed to being needy at times. It's a complex stew of backstory crashing into doubt and fear. I know this about myself, and I don't accept it without fighting against it. I work on it because I know it causes my wife a bit of stress when I am, in fact, needy.

This is perhaps ironic, but it is what it is. To be needy, and to have that evoke a harsh response that makes one even more needy, because that response feeds the very insecurities that originated it… this is the very definition of insanity. Mine, in this case.

Sometimes I can't read her. Like all of us, she occasionally goes silent, seems distracted, or perhaps something else is going on for her. Maybe she's deep in thought about something other than me. That's one of her favorite responses, that it's not always about me.

Then again, maybe it is about me. That is sometimes true, as well.

But until she comes clean and explains, I can't truly know the cause of her silence or distraction. Certainly, she has a right to those states and moods. We all do. But I confess, when it happens I experience a sense of doubt and resultant stress. There is something in the air, even if I'm not the cause of it, and even if I have simply misread her.

And so, sometimes I ask what is wrong.

Now, if it was as the first time I'd asked her that question, and because she is a very reasonable woman, I would get a polite and calm answer. "Nothing is wrong" with perhaps a smile and pat on the head to assure me. Then again, maybe something is wrong but she's not ready to confront it. Maybe it's none of my business, which in a marriage is always a complex explanation.

But now, after twenty years of these questions, which arise from twenty years of her occasionally going silent—notice the two-party dance with this issue—I don't usually get a patient response. I get something else, something I describe as a *snap*. On occasion that snap is ferocious, beyond the degree of the transgression itself.

Which is what I call an over-reaction. And thus, the evening is ruined.

So let's dissect this moment.

My asking is a product of a collision of two needs, which can swap places in line: a genuine concern for her state, for her peace of mind, and then, a genuine need for my own reassurance that we're okay. That I'm okay. That I haven't somehow, unknowingly—or in rarer cases, absolutely in the knowledge that I may have hit the wrong button with her—triggered something that will at some point boil over into a confrontation.

Now let's flip this to her point of view. There may or may not actually be something wrong. Most of the time, there isn't. She has an active mind, she jumps from thing to thing faster than most people take their next breath. So what she hears—because I've done it so often—is me being needy again. Me imagining things.

Or worse, that I'm intruding into her mind space.

Now let's step back and look at the deeper picture for us both.

Neither of us feels safe when this happens.

It's not safe for me to ask. Which means, every time I feel a genuine need to inquire, I am stepping into risk. I'm likely going to get a harsh, impatient response. Where I'm thinking I'm being a concerned husband, she thinks I'm being a nosy and needy husband. And on her end, she's not safe to go to an introspective, quiet space in my presence, because I'm going to shatter the silence with that question—*are you okay, is anything wrong?*—again.

This is just an example in a thick volume of examples in any relationship. We all have little things that bother us, recurring behaviors and actions that drive our partner crazy. Too much, too often, and it all melts into a big boiled pot of discontent.

In regard to our loving each other and being the best version of ourselves for each other, there is nothing wrong with the question, and there is nothing wrong with her checking out on me once in a while. But what *is* wrong, from both sides, is to compromise the sense of safety of our partner, by injecting risk and harsh consequences into the equation.

I bet any of us could create a short list of things that define moments, actions, behaviors and responses where we feel less than safe in our relationship. Things we want to talk about but can't. Things we want to do but can't. Things that should happen that don't. Things we desire but are denied. The list of possibilities is long and wide, and it defines the landscape of perfectly normal relationships in all forms and cultures.

But those are just the daily potholes we must navigate.

Sometimes the prospect of feeling safe in our relationship can be even darker. Dangerous, even.

When we speak of safety within a relationship, we don't usually think of bad moods and harsh reactions. We land on the unthinkable, the stuff of 9-1-1 calls and interventions. Both fall under this header, but the context of each—potentially toxic in either case—is quite different indeed.

I don't need to tell you where your lines are in this regard.

And what the consequences of crossing them might be. Only you know what you or your partner are capable of. I'm talking about the nature of any unhealthy, risky responses to the moments that try our patience or tolerance, deserved or not.

I'm also talking about tolerating abuse on any level, and how this makes the silent victim a party to the dysfunction, if not to the same degree as the abuser, then at least as a contributor to the erosion of peace between you. I tell my wife that when she snaps at me, deserved or not, it is no different than a literal backhand across the jaw. The consequences are, in terms of damage to the spirit, very much the same.

That one got her attention. She thought on it, long and hard. And it doesn't happen much anymore, precisely because—this being the ironic epilogue to this little anecdote—I felt safe in speaking my mind.

Who is right or wrong isn't the issue. It's how we respond to stress that becomes the issue on both sides of an incident. You could be completely justified in flying off the handle—most people who fly too far off that handle do indeed feel warranted in doing so—but when that happens you are creating an unsafe condition and environment for your spouse.

Do it frequently enough, and you could end up being dead right. As in, watching as your spouse heads out the door.

Some things you can discuss calmly, lovingly, and some problems you cannot solve. As with all this material, the point here is awareness. I am not qualified, nor is it my intention, to instruct anyone on how to work out substantive problems that are bigger than your ability to cope or dissect, much less address.

The point is this: some sort of effort is called for when your safety, or that of your partner, is in question. If you can't work it out, find a professional who can. And do it now, before another moment of discomfort and fear darkens your doorway.

2. The Realm of Authenticity

The last thing you need right now is a lecture on the value of communication—lots of it—within a relationship. It resides near the top on any list of the obvious, right between "keep your eye on the ball" and "karma's a bitch."

Communications on any front are always a qualitative proposition, driven by a quantitative expectation. In other words, you have to get in the game, and once there, you need to play it at a high level.

Perhaps a bad analogy there. Because this isn't a game at all. Communicating effectively, lovingly and selflessly—all three being different approaches—is the mother of all make-or-break domestic skills. True authenticity is the key to making it work.

Often it is the obviousness of it that gets in the way.

We take for granted what it means to be authentic. We don't value the need for it in the day-to-day of our lives, reverting to what is best described as a sort of autopilot mode. Speaking your mind in the moment. Sometimes we defend how we communicate—ranting, raving, interrupting, not listening, a lack of empathy—by rationalizing we are really *that* angry. Sometimes with good cause. In such moments we find the high-road clouded by other things, the pressures of real life, infiltrated by nagging little resentments, secret feelings of need or disappointment, or personal agendas.

Or, too often, just plain old bad habits. Perhaps you've never learned what authenticity even means within the process of communicating with you partner.

These things conspire to imbue our relational communications with shades and nuances that may be counter-productive.

There is a dark side to authenticity, as well. Let's say one of you has a certifiable anger management problem. You explode at the slightest provocation, or even if warranted, your response compromises the safety of the other. That party might argue that this response is, in fact, authentic. At least for them. This is a situation that requires intervention, I haven't met a couple yet who can sit down and talk their way through a bona fide psychological problem.

Awareness, driven by a commitment to become your best self for your partner, can lead you to an appropriate strategy of response.

Actually, I'm being too polite here. Let me say this more accurately: sometimes the way a couple communicates, when it comes to the level of authenticity—because genuine aggression can be as authentic as anything else—is the primary factor in their unhappiness and ultimate failure.

Get it fixed. Before it destroys the union between you.

And so we are left to manage authenticity on more than one front.

What we say, and how we say it. From a position of being right, wrong or something in between.

But perhaps there is another front, as well. This one differentiating between the intention of what we say and do from the consequential power of it. The effect, if you will. Optimally, authenticity is the place from which intention should come. Are we coming from love, or are we coming from a place of either defensiveness or of striking the first blow? Is there an agenda in tow? True authenticity challenges us to notice and eliminate anything that colors our message beyond what the words seem to say, even when such intentions support our own agenda.

Sarcasm, anger, condescension, impatience, volume, profanity, triangulation, belittlement, arrogance... all of these are the stuff of inauthenticity. And yet, at least some of those are honest emotions, made risky by the fact that any sense of righteous indignation becomes, in itself, a less than authentic means of expressing one's self. How we manage and juggle the sentiments behind our words and intentions is the key to effectiveness.

And always, love itself is the secret sauce that keeps us safe from these complexities, as well as effective in the exchanges themselves. Love is what holds up the mirror that can save us. To be abusive is not love, it is lazy self-service and cowardice.

The silence of inauthenticity.

Silence is not always golden. Any time you are fighting without saying anything—the silent treatment as a means of expressing your anger and resentment; you feel the need to hit back, and silence is your choice—even if you choose to bottle it up, you are relating in a less than authentic way. And doing damage each time it happens.

You can handle tough situations with patience, love, empathy and a strategic sense of what might work... or not. The key is to understand that this is a moment of choice for you, even if it appears your partner has already made a choice.

Authenticity requires courage and a keen sense of self-awareness.

There is a price to pay for it when you are the only one in the room being authentic. At that point the decision is more about what is productive and loving, rather than authenticity for authenticity's sake.

In other words, pick your battles.

Karma is more a bitch than a force that seeks to create balance.

In our moments of inauthenticity, we tend to think we're getting away with something. But usually we're not, not even a little. Too often the unspoken is the loudest noise in the room. Lack of authenticity sows the seeds of discontent on many levels, because it tends to escalate, and soon dishonesty and outright cruelty—often masquerading as a defense mechanism in a *the-best-defense-is-a-good-offense* world—becomes the dominant tenor between you.

You can abort this vicious circle of inauthenticity by acknowledging it, and using the power of true authenticity, seasoned by courage and vulnerability, to reinvent your best self for your partner, and vice versa. When you can achieve that in the most stressful and trying moments between you, then you are truly already on the road to bliss.

Because eventually you'll get that in return. The trick is to wait it out until that wonderful quid pro quo kicks in.

Of course, we're human, and stuff happens. That is a mantra that never changes in a relationship. And thus, this becomes a journey that never reaches an ultimate port of call, demanding our attention and best loving effort each and every day.

Which is what you committed to, by the way, back at the beginning of your love affair.

The efficacy of the intention to live and communicate authentically depends on how you define your degree of authenticity in any given moment. On a treadmill, 80-percent effort may feel like you're going all out to the point of collapse, when in fact you are leaving a significant percentage of your potential untapped. That last 20-percent is new, uncharted territory for you.

It could be, too, that you've been less than authentic for so long, trapped in a mutual game of spinning and editing your exterior self to fit the moment—perhaps hiding behind a defense mechanism that has served you thus far, or so you believe—that you wouldn't recognize your truest, most authentic self if you were strapped to a CIA-certified, drug-enhanced lie detector device.

We've all known people like this.

People whose every word, every posture, every response, is imbued with something that is less than authentic. An agenda is fully apparent, to appear and be a certain way—smarter, tougher, more worldly, more informed, less impacted, more impacted, or just plain superior to everyone else in the room—or in general for reasons that are more hubris than issue-specific. The person doing it may have begun to believe their own lies, or they have used it as a shield for so long they don't really know how else to act.

If, as you read this you're wincing on the inside right now, that's good. You may be recognizing yourself in that paragraph, and hopefully beginning to realize it becomes a death spiral, rather than a means of getting by. Such recognition becomes a huge first step toward the authenticity you seek, or should be seeking.

But as someone on the receiving end of such inauthenticity, you see through it in an instant, and almost every time. The only person in the room who believes what the narcissist is selling is the purveyor of the illusion. But do you say anything? Probably not. No need to stir things up.

Within our primary relationships this all becomes a slippery slope on both sides of the conversation.

When authenticity is a baseline assumption, tested and proven over time, the result is intimacy. Pure, unthreatening, hopeful intimacy. Within authentic two-way communications we know we are being heard, and what we are putting forth is completely true and stripped of B.S. and agenda. It is exactly what we want and need our partner to hear and feel.

In a few pages we'll be discussing just that: intimacy. Which goes to show that all of these realms end up converging, creating a sum which is truly in excess of the parts.

The issue of authenticity spills over from passive and conflicted moments into loving and intimate moments, as well. Authenticity is the magic dust of being in love, because there is no smoke screen, no holding back, to overt intention to withhold or to hurt.

Every conversation you have becomes both an opportunity and a test of your level of authenticity. You'll quickly realize this to be true, even when there is a period of adjustment. Because if this is a major shift for you it'll be as obvious and even awkward as a sudden preference for social nudity—this is more an emotional nudity between you—which of course would freeze your partner in his/her tracks.

But hang in there with it. Talk about this very thing, the degree and nature of your mutual authenticity. Ask for it. Notice it. Give positive feedback when you sense it. Be grateful for it. And most of all, continue to practice and give authenticity, because it truly is a gift, not just to your partner, but to yourself and your relationship, which is almost like a third entity that the two of you are entrusted and committed to care for.

False fronts, agendas, attitudes, bluster, cowardice, indirectness... these are the fumblings of couples who struggle. Authenticity, on the other hand, while never perfect, is the vehicle for couples who truly seek to become the best version of themselves, to achieve the best possible relationship experience possible.

And thus, carried by that vehicle, bliss becomes a possible dream.

3. The Realm of Inner Demons

This one, as it relates to relationship maintenance and repair, is for the most part best left to professionals with credentials hanging on their office wall. They are certainly doing a booming business, one that has only touched the surface of the market for what they do.

We all need fixing. We all would benefit from help. And we all play a role in our own therapy.

So let's talk about *that*.

In the previous chapter I mentioned legitimate temper and anger management issues. I mention it again here to illustrate how an inner demon, which is the soul of an anger problem, manifests within the other realms of relationship. Beating back an inner demon is like killing a weed at the root. The garden can now grow unencumbered.

The realm of inner demons is for all of us, because we all bring *stuff* to the relationship party. Very few of us grew up in a television sitcom with the Cleavers as our neighbors (younger readers take note: *Leave it to Beaver* was the *Full House* of the 1960s, long before *All in the Family* had the courage to get real about human imperfection). The values and priorities of the generation that raised us differed wildly from those we now know best serve us in each of the realms of relationship discussed here.

Those inner demons may have DNA that connects to that prior generation upbringing. Dad taught you that real men don't show emotion. Mom taught you that women should know their place, and that the place she, at least, has accepted is suspect. And now, in a world in which all this has been proven to be complete and utter crap, you find yourself wrestling with the ghosts of your past.

The problem and the goal are both simple, and offered with respect to the truth that we all have things buried within us, often defining us, that we need to recognize and do battle with. Those inner demons, in all their forms, become the problem.

The supreme goal, the most effective strategy of anything Dr. Phil or his peers could put on the table, is this: we need to recognize the bullshit—dysfunction—that infiltrates our beliefs, behaviors, actions and world view, and once recognized, begin the work of eradicating it from our lives.

Bullshit is the enemy.

Skewed beliefs, negative habits and the fears and unreasonableness of our lives remain omnipresent. These things define us. And too often, hold us back from living as the best possible version of ourselves.

I realize how simplistic this sounds. Self-inflicted toxins are sometimes woefully simple.

The eradication of B.S. from your life can begin the very next time you have a discussion or an argument with your partner. Or the next time you socialize with others. The next time you take a trip. The next time you discipline your children. Even the next time you make love. Even the next time you are about to express an opinion.

We see it everywhere.

We all have a certain sphere of awareness of the people in our lives, folks we know well enough to see through polite exteriors to perceive an inner landscape where demons reside and breed. It would be easy to begin a litany of the dysfunction I've witnessed, and rationalize it as an example necessary to a robust discussion of this topic.

But before I shine a light on anyone else, I should begin with an inventory of the pure and utter B.S. that runs me.

Which is precisely what I'm suggesting you do for yourself, as well.

My mother was a functioning alcoholic.

By functioning, I mean that every three to ten weeks or so she'd go on a bender and turn into Joan Crawford with a hanger. The other weeks she was simply intolerable, but not drunk.

Everything in my childhood that transpired within pouring distance of alcohol remains as a dark memory. Never once did my parents leave the house to socialize with others, or even just the two of them—which was even rarer—that didn't turn into a raging throw down. My mother couldn't stop at one drink, and by the second she was a slobbering mess of cruel insults and manic raving, strangling my father with resentment-driven old tapes, none of which were ever clear to me as I listened to them go at each other. Certainly, her own backstory had driven her to some chaotic abyss, which alcohol only served to exacerbate.

To this day I cannot summon a single memory of them laughing. Not one. Or even having a genuine, non-confrontational conversation, for that matter. Somehow my sister turned out to be a lovely angel of a woman. It wasn't that she'd tucked it all away, deep inside, she just forgave them and moved on quicker and better than I could.

I had written here about other traces of damage done, but my wife asked me to take them out. At first I resisted—total transparency being my goal—but it meant something to her, so I did it.

That's an example of what I'm talking about. Giving your partner the win whenever you can.

Meanwhile, I burned through two tough marriages and a long resume of jobs, a revolving door of friends, all precisely because of the same parental modeling, at least in part. I'm not blaming them for my issues, just taking inventory of where they came from. We tend to emulate not just what has been shown to us—that's too simple—but rather, the message of that modeling.

I told you it was complicated. Professional intervention is always best when one submits to the realization they aren't in full command of what runs them.

My own son, God bless him, on the cusp of leaving home for college, had the courage and respect to actually sit me down and discuss one of my demons with me. The judgmental one. He may or may not have experimented with alcohol in high school, but I'm pretty sure he wasn't out there partying in the basements of other parents who were away for a weekend and came home to a depleted liquor cabinet. A DUI was never going to be on his prep resume. He just wasn't that kid, and I was proud of that.

So when he told me that he intended to drink socially in college, a thousand miles to the south of where I would sit in judgment, I was actually relieved. I didn't wish him the same isolated experience that I had in those formative years as a baseball player and a college student. He said he didn't want to do his partying on the sly, he wanted to honor the integrity of our relationship, and that I should trust him in this.

I realized I was more proud of that courage and authenticity than I would be of him sitting on the social sidelines, which was my backstory and the outcome of more than a few of my own inner demons. He remains the most squared away, consistently happy, morally optimized and genuinely likeable human being I know... and he still drinks like a college freshman from time to time.

So what do I know.

To the extent I actually do know, it is because I take pause to inventory and study the inner demons that continue to plague me. The confrontation of which, says my wife, contributes to me being a tolerable husband in a wonderful marriage. I also know that much work remains to be done.

My wife arrived in our marriage twenty-years ago with a fond relationship to partying. As did the friends from her prior life, which bore little resemblance to mine. They were *normal*. Party party party. They had grown up together as young couples with young kids, cutting loose on weekends, guys in one room lying about their golf game and bragging up a storm about their jobs, while the wives were off playing cards and chatting it up in another room, much of it at the expense of their unknowing husbands.

As for me, in those early years I was that guy in the Kenny Loggins song: "... *never got high, oh he was a sorry guy.*" I wasn't actually sorry, but I certainly was alone a lot.

My list of bullshit remains long and varied.

I don't believe I'm any more flawed than anyone else in my life—I certainly don't believe I'm remotely more squared away, either—but it can certainly feel that way when one looks inward to examine the landscape where those inner demons are scheming for control while flashing still frames from the past.

Like the one where my father was lying on the couch after we brought him home from a three-day hospital stay, eighty surgical stitches fresh in his neck, holding his spine together where a cervical disc used to be, with my mother leaning over him, spilling Early Times mixed with her spittle on his chest, and him trying to raise up and slap the glass away, missing badly before falling forward over the coffee table to the floor, his hands clasping his neck... her laughing at him...

... and then the next thing I remember was her head wedged between the wall and the ceiling at the end of my arms, because I was a nineteen-year old professional athlete strong enough to do just that, a young man who just couldn't handle what he had just seen.

And then my Dad got screaming mad at *me* for what I'd done.

To this day—decades later—I don't do conflict all that well.

I am a classic conflict-avoider. I take way too much grief, and then I snap... way too hard. I don't suffer bullies or idiots, both of which are out there in abundance. I tell my wife: *I never met a drunk woman I thought was sexy, and I never met a drunk guy I want to hang with.* I care too much what people think. I'll avoid a room full of people I don't know at all costs, unless I am teaching or giving a keynote address, in which case I'm completely comfortable. I'm much more at ease speaking to an audience of hundreds than I am standing in a room confronted with the prospect of chit-chat.

In those and other respects, I am a walking case study in contrast and contradiction. All of it connected in some way to my backstory, be it childhood or those early formative socialization years.

Still working on all of it. Getting better at some of it. The principle of authenticity, fueled by a keener awareness of my inner twisted wires, makes better choices more readily available.

So I believe I'm qualified to talk about inner demons from a user point of view.

All these years have taught me that none of it licenses anything on my own roster of B.S. And yet, the inner demons are always there, trying to claw their way out of my id and into my life. The degree to which they succeed defines my weakness and my ignorance, both of which must be reversed before the screaming in our head goes away.

That reversal, by the way, is born of stepping into fear in pursuit of a higher, more loving goal, which some would describe as courage. I like to think of it as necessary. A better-to-best version of ourselves is always available, even if an inner demon is trying to make us look away.

I have a #10 wife, a son of whom I couldn't be more proud, and a loving extended family, all of whom are rooting for me, even though they have long ago forgotten anything about my backstory. I am grateful, to some extent, for that backstory, because it has led me to this level of introspection, even to the writing of this book.

Inner demons almost always back down when you look them in the eye and tell them you are no longer listening.

I know, and you probably know, flaming narcissists; misogynists; cowards; control freaks; loners; stoners; the pathologically insecure; the morally bankrupt; the unbalanced and the confused; those who believe as if *it's-all-about-me*; the irretrievably stuck; folks who absolutely cannot be and have never been wrong; people who are completely controlled by fear; the terminally lazy; men who outwardly lay claim to literally being the king of their castle and women who demonstrate a compensating sense of superiority; people with selective memory; those with pretentious tastes; people hiding behind a mask; others behind walls of their own construction; people who cannot forgive, nor can they forget, yet never apologize; those who say *that's just me, take me as I am because I'll never change* as if that's a good thing; those who justify tunnel vision because *that's how dad did things*; and those who could not spell i-n-t-i-m-a-c-y if you gave them a gift-wrapped first edition Webster's with a gilded page-mark in the right place.

When intimacy scares the holy hell out of you, that's your inner demons doing a dance on the grave of your grasp on relationship reality.

Much of this is simple laziness, fueled by ignorance.

Because challenging the status quo created by our inner demons, which are fortified by the collision with the inner demons of the person we live with, is daunting, uncharted, terrifying work.

It is work I am hereby suggesting you undertake. If you are truly interested in an abnormal level of happiness and fulfillment, it is work you must engage with. Because bullshit—yours—is the primary obstacle in that pursuit.

For the most part all those folks I just blindly called out are perfectly fine human beings, reasonably happy (or so they have rationalized), yet visibly struggling from time to time with the stuff that torments them. As are we all.

They are content, resigned to autopilot, contributing to a collective divorce rate telling us that half of first marriages and 70-percent of second and third marriages will fail. There is no data on how many of the survivors are swallowing a tanker full of compromise and resentment to remain together, thus resigned to the death of, or comatose state of, what was once a bright dream. That said, I'm sure the statistic on those in hot pursuit or attainment of actual bliss is a miniscule shard of demographical data, indeed.

Just this week, my wife and I met with friends who decided to notice.

They'd had enough. After twenty years of perfectly normal attrition of their relationship, they confronted their autopilot status and acknowledged the risk, the inevitable forecast of failure if they simply stayed that course. They had the courage to stand up and look in a mirror, the one where inner demons laugh at us from the background. They decided to be different, to shed their crap, to proactively cultivate intimacy and re-engage in truly authentic communications. And to do it with patience and tolerance for imperfection, which is also inevitable.

They had sat on those feelings for years, but finally summoned the courage—motivated by sensing the proximity of a breaking point—to have the conversation.

Bliss is always a product of playing the long game, every time. But it is also dependent on that course-changing conversation, commencing a series of equally critical maintenance and growth-oriented conversations and commitments to follow.

And for the first time in years, they gleefully admit, they are happy again. Not because they have been suddenly rendered perfect, but because hope has been resurrected. The entire baseline tonality of their relationship is different. B.S. is no longer welcome in their house.

Because of this shift, the love they once shared had been snatched from the jaws of statistical probability and poured over them, saturating every interaction and every quiet thought.

What's different now is the *context* of their relationship.

Most of us know what our inner demons are and how they manifest in our life, usually with the unmistakable stench of bullshit.

Acknowledge that this is a choice.

It is available now, in this moment, the instant you put down this book and look your partner, your beautiful partner, in the eye.

Try it. Tell your partner that you love her/him. Tell her/him that you are sorry if you've been less than loving, less than giving, more into you than the-two-of-you. You may get a look of utter confusion. You may be poking a bear, which is usually something that has to happen anyway.

Do this, and you will have walked through a door that can change everything. Just don't take your inner demons with you as you cross that threshold.

After that initial acknowledgement, what you do about it becomes the next choice, be it an engagement with a professional therapist or some course of emotional rehabilitation. Or, you've simply made the decision—and issued an invitation—to love again...

... unconditionally, generously, and courageously.

Tell your inner demons to buzz off. Start putting your partner first, instead of them.

4. The Realm of Tone

We are always in communication with our partners, and in two ways. The enlightened lover manages both of them, never allowing either to descend into autopilot, where message and meaning may become diffused and misinterpreted.

The first is the verbal way in which we communicate. What we say, and how we say it. This is the day-to-day currency of living together and loving in harmony, and there are some very real ways we can screw it up.

The other way is more subtle and nuanced. More a non-verbal strategy. These are the ways we show our love—or our impatience—rather than how we verbalize it.

First up… the tone we impart to our words.

Tone and attitude speak volumes.

The loss of a kinder, gentler tone between you isn't an inevitable phase of a relationship.

But it can become inevitable when the unwelcome tone and attitude is accepted as, well, acceptable. The more it happens without consequences, the more the offending party believes they can get away with it. Because from their point of view it does no harm.

The offender writes it off as a moment, and when that moment is over the world returns to normal. The wounded partner, however, registers it on an expanding scorecard of dissatisfaction.

Often—and this will sound trite, but it's true—it's simply that you forgot to be nice. The pressure of a situation or moment, perhaps seasoned by provocation or resentment, trumps your ability to be your best self, inciting you to speak from a place of frustration rather than a place of love.

Truly, no one ever really gets away with tone that is toxic, cruel and unfair because it is out of balance with the transgression.

Tone is often an insidious, gradual descent in the level of patience and the degree of discernable irritation either party displays. It becomes a vicious circle, tone begetting tone, and it can too easily flare into something more than a cranky moment.

Tone can also by symptomatic of larger issues. I know that when I am on the receiving end of an impatient and out of balance rebuke or harsh barb, I hang onto it for hours, maybe the whole day, forcing me—because my wife has forgotten it within moments—to be less than authentic as I stuff the resentment back down into the dark crevice of that scorecard. In that blacked out period of resentful response, my mind goes to dark places, completely shifting the lens through which I regard my wife and our partnership. It's overblown, but in the moment it feels very real.

If you're thinking this is less than healthy, that's the point.

The consequence of negative tone, fair or otherwise, remain as something toxic in the air between you.

Less-than-playful sarcasm, bubbling up resentment, even simple impatience, is like releasing a noxious gas into the domestic environment. It immediately attacks the tissue of emotional bonding. Repeated and unbalanced negativity soaks into the relationship at a cellular level, and over time, becomes the norm.

Living with someone, even in the presence of professed love, is always challenging at times. The risk of occasionally lashing out with something insensitive or outright cruelty is a matter of intention, intensity and frequency, all three of which can and should be managed. Because the consequences can be the silent killer of affection, leading to larger and darker consequences.

If the unspoken truth is that your partner thinks you are a bit of a bitch, too often—or a bit of an asshole, too often—then indeed, it is happening too often. There is already blood in the water of your relationship. It then becomes an issue of how much can be tolerated, and the hope of resolution that is or isn't on the table.

You not only have a habit to break, but a wound that requires healing.

Earlier I discussed the risky nature of a relationship that has gone on autopilot. Some couples experience autopilot as a constant tone of affection—this should always be the goal—but frankly, based on observation, I believe it is more common when autopilot describes the expectation and defensive volleying of thoughtless jabs and insensitive remarks.

You've been around other couples who do this. Snarky sparks fly, as if unaware and uncaring about who is there to see. It's uncomfortable to experience, because you wonder what resides behind it. When both parties react with knee jerk emotional jabs and counterpunches as a matter of course, as a defense that has evolved into a hit-first offense, it is symptomatic of other issues that, like a spot on the skin, may have roots extending to dark places.

Too often, when this back-and-forth gets out of hand, the issues underlying and prompting impatience and resentment tend to fall behind the more immediate dysfunction of the toxicity itself. Getting up in the morning feels like stepping into a ring, where you know and expect to both defend and deliver blows that are meant to inflict pain. You feel obliged to defend and strike back, or strike first—the best defense being a good offense—because if you don't, you'll get pummeled.

You need to talk.

Hopefully, this is behavior that can be mitigated, and over time, remedied by a simple acknowledgement of it, leading to an authentic and mutual agreement to tone it down. If both parties agree the air between them smells more like the lobby of a divorce lawyer than it does a happy home occupied by people committed to the peace and joy of the other, then actually talking about how you talk—or don't talk, which is another form of toxicity—will soon disarm the conflict, at least for the time being. Apologies and renewed commitments can then fill the space between you, without the stench of cynicism getting in the way.

Sometimes the stress of these moments can be legitimately bigger than you.

If there is truly an issue driving the harsh words, sharp jabs or impatience, then another kind of conversation becomes necessary. Or counseling, if the issue is complex or painful beyond your ability to have that conversation productively. Bad behavior always warrants consequences, which in healthy relationships must be something other than punishment.

In a healthy relationship, punishment and revenge are never part of the dialogue.

An apology is the most effective form of acknowledgement.

When you see the wrong response to your tone evident in your partner's eyes, quickly admit you were playing too rough. You were insensitive. You were distracted by something that has nothing to do with her/him, or if it does, is better dealt with in another way. Because it is the lack of sensitivity that hurts as much as the nature of the barb itself, and if you can catch it quickly it shows you are more aware than you are entitled.

Apologize. It is the miracle drug of relationships, and it can work immediately. The lack of an appropriate and timely apology stings every bit as much as the verbal backhand itself. Which means you've struck two blows, not just one.

Especially when the issue is simply an unfortunate choice of words or tone. Go even one better—punctuate your apology with a hug. No matter what the issue, if your tone was the first punch thrown, then you are in the wrong. The apology is on you.

My wife and I discovered this early in our relationship, which began from the embedded behaviors and expectations that carried over from each of our previous relationships.

My wife will tell you, she's a kidder.

But that is sometimes a smoke-screen for a darker intention.

She is a formidable foe in getting the best of someone playing the dark game of emotional one-on-one. She can dish it, and it can be either funny or dangerous—sometimes both—the latter usually delivered within an illusion of an intent to be funny. This *gotcha*! tonality somewhat defined her prior marriage, which had twenty-seven years of embedding behind it when I became the guy in her bed. She had married early in life, as had her closest friends, all of them from the same blue collar neighborhood in which the parents practiced what I call "the joust" as a matter of course—those old tapes are hard to erase—and the kids took it forward into their own lives with a nearly one hundred percent divorce rate.

One couple made it through, though, and it is precisely because they understand the role of tone along with the long list of things that also either fortify or erode a relationship.

As for me, I came from a home run by an alcoholic mother and an ex-marine drill instructor who, when he reached his quite reasonable limit, became someone who was less than reasonable. I remember the police at our front door, I remember visiting my mother in the hospital, telling the nurses what a monster she was married to. I clung to, and continue to cling to, a deeply rooted distaste and intolerance for friction, any friction, even when friction is warranted, even when one of us thought they were merely being cute, because flipping crap and reacting with impatience is, for some, considered cute.

So one day my wife found herself slinging some serious attitude my way—innocent needling, she thought, the stuff wives and husbands do, from her experience—as a matter of course. Prior to that day I had laughed it off. But on this occasion I perceived a particularly mean spirit to it.

Remember that I confessed up front in this book that I love her desperately, which is a significant clue to how I feel about even playful domestic warfare and the crossfire of witty torment: I don't like it. Not a bit, not for a moment. Save your *get-the-best-of-the-other-guy* trash talk and wit-wars for your card games and golf outings, I'm just not that guy.

That day, in the midst of this, as I was sensing a sharpness she may or may not have intended, she suddenly observed the expression on my face. Her method had been to escalate these little war of words, waiting for me to engage, or if I seemed offended then jumping on *that*, but on this day she realized she was having a party of one. She was escalating all by herself. I was just looking at her with an expression she described as that of someone who was more puppy dog hurt and confused than someone ready to suit up and fight back.

I remember what she said without pausing to even consider her words (something that, in retrospect, I wish she would have done before the moment transpired... then again, the result became a touchstone for us going forward), right after covering her mouth with the palm of her hand: "Oh my god... this isn't you! You don't do this... you don't deserve this! I don't have to do this sh*t anymore!"

The ghosts of past lives are reluctant to leave us.

And since then, because we continue to be human and, thus, occasionally irritate the crap out of each other—and because, she's a kidder, and you can take the kidder out of the old 'hood, but you can't take the old 'hood out of the kidder—we remind each other of this difference between us, this higher sensibility. Which usually accomplishes one of two things: it silences the gunfire, and/or it launches a deeper discussion that is issue-driven, rather than fueled by anger, hurt feelings, sarcasm and resentment.

Bottom line: watch your tone.

Because you're playing with fire when tone goes south. The kind of fire that consumes slowly, from within, over time.

Watch your tone even when you are on the cusp of anger or impatience. *Especially* when you are on the precipice of anger or impatience, even if it is prompted by some level of what you believe to be legitimate resentment. Think of your words—any words, at any time—as a means of expression of your love. Or, when used as weapons, the opposite. Love is certainly sometimes by necessity critical or disapproving. To shy away from confrontation is to hide from the truth, which is its own form of toxicity. But love is a 24-7, vows-to-graveyard proposition without timeouts.

We need to love our partners in the tough moments.

Tone is what happens when we don't feel in complete control of a moment.

Don't pick up a bat and join the street fight. Don't try to out-heckle the heckler. Rather, adopt a more sincere tone, thoughtful and issue-driven, that is never intended as a weapon or a message, infused with a commitment to keep the toxins between you at a minimum.

Tone can be the tip of a colder iceberg. Don't hesitate to get help when the conversations become bigger than either of you. When one of you can't handle the truth. When one of you can't hear it, can't be wrong, can't be challenged.

Make your words count. Even when you're not counting.

5. The Languages of Love

In his 1995 book *"The Five Languages of Love: How to Express Heartfelt Commitment to Your Mate,"* author Gary Chapman tells us there are five languages of love: gifts, spending quality time, words of affirmation, acts of service, and physical touch.

Having just dealt with how we wield our words, let's look at how these other four are issues of degree, things we are already doing. And thus, they become variables we can control, rather than allowing them to control us.

We've all had to deal with the consequences on both levels.

Not long ago my wife and I faced a major life change.

Not to bore you with the details… just think of the '08 mortgage crash, concurrent with a stock market dive. Our house had sunk below its previous value, the one used to collateralize our mortgage, resulting in the need to move and occupy what had been our second home in the sun, which was thankfully mortgage-free though less than half the square footage and over a thousand miles from family and friends.

In other words, a curveball that became a knock-down pitch. We had been living a dream, and then we woke up at the sound of thunder. Or better put, by a cold splash of reality.

To pre-empt and buffer the emotional roller coaster ride ahead, we scheduled a couple of sessions with a counselor we had seen before. Normally, when someone says they're seeing a marriage counselor, people tend to assign some dark meaning to it—not the case with us. Proactive preventative maintenance was our thing. We'd seen this brilliant fellow before—because the reality hits just keep on coming—and we were returning to him now simply to get some tools to help us weather the move and support each other more fully along the way.

And, to not allow the pressure and darkness of the ride to drag us down into a place from which we could not recover.

I highly recommend you consider doing this (seeing a professional, that is). Think of it as going to the gym to get strong as opposed to going to the doctor to get well.

Anyhow, in the course of discussing how we were faring as this collateralized house of cards was falling all around us, the issue of communication styles came up, as it always does at some point in the relationship counseling conversation. In our case, the issue wasn't who loved and who didn't, but rather, how that love was expressed to each other. And that's where a big whopping *ah-hah!* moment arrived.

We were at opposite ends of the spectrum on this one. Not a right vs. wrong spectrum, but a potato-tomato difference.

I'm verbal. I tell her how much I love her, how beautiful she is, how much I desire her... and I do it frequently. Like, ridiculously often, with complete authenticity, because that's what it is.

My wife, on the other hand, is someone who speaks a very different language of love. She is a doer. A caretaker. She demonstrates her love by doing things for us, and for me. Not so much as signs of affection—no poems or flowers—but in the form of caring for the house and our daily necessities, including my laundry, spiced with little touches of the unexpected.

I'd never thought of laundry that way. I can take or leave laundry, I assign no meaning to it, and I'm more than happy to do my own. But to her, when she does the laundry she is *speaking* to me in her preferred language of love. Which is to say, she is loving me.

To appreciate this, you need to know that I'm no old school gender roles guy, nor am I a romantic fool (okay, maybe a little). I do nearly all of the grocery shopping. About half the time I clear the table and load the dishwasher, especially if guests are involved. I know where the iron is kept. I make the bed for us every morning. I have my little chores, unassigned yet assumed, and she has hers, in both cases by choice. And in both cases, much appreciated. (My wife, after reading this, wants you to know she cooks frequently, that our division of labor is more than equal, rather than the hero I just made myself out to be; that said, she won't let me dust, because I suck at it.)

The difference in how we view this, though, is important: I do these things because I want to help out. Because it is fair. I don't for a moment think any of it is *her* job, or as a favor, something that I'm heroically off-loading from her plate. It's not a surprise gesture, just me trying to pull my weight. It is a partnering thing, rather than a pandering thing.

She, on the other hand, takes care of me and our home as an expression of love. Including my laundry. I try, and never completely succeed, to thank her regularly. She's better at that part, she thanks me every day for the bed.

It's interesting to note that when either of us is out of town, leaving the other alone in our home, none of this stuff gets done by the one left behind. No bed, no laundry, no grocery shopping. That's telling.

Because at the end of the day, it's all about each other, more than the work. This is the most important thing to appreciate, over and above the perceived value of the acts themselves.

We each try to speak the other's language when we can—me doing things, her saying things.

This works for us because, now more than ever we recognize the different love languages being spoken in our home. We both are capable of speaking both languages, and we do on occasion, but each of us has a favorite, even a default tongue on this issue.

Every once in a while, usually with a cuddle of some kind, she'll tell me how lucky she feels to have a husband that says these amazing things to her. That's her speaking my language of love. And just as often, I try to find the right moment to *show* her how much I appreciate the great care she takes of me by finding something to do for her, even if it is the simplest act of domestic proactivity.

It works. It's not contrived, not a mantra, not a strategy. It's not to gain something in return. It's the outcome of the sum of the choices we have made about who we are together, and what that demands of us as individuals engaged in a two-part conspiracy to live in marital bliss, with two different love languages being spoken in our home.

Communication is the currency of love.

No matter what language it comes in. Learn to speak the language your partner notices and appreciates—don't demand that she speaks yours exclusively—and you'll find the love returned in kind.

Effective and frequent communication is like great sex. Once you know what your partner desires, likes and needs, the smart and giving lover goes there, happily, frequently, and with passion.

6. The Realm of Conflict Resolution

So far we've covered five *behavioral* Realms of Relationship. Stuff that is fundamental to simply getting along together. These are skills-oriented contexts, areas that you're good or bad at to some extent, in either direction.

Better to be good at them. Because they inform what comes next.

These five realms are like speed, strength and agility to an athlete. None ensure that you will be good at the game itself, but they're essential to getting there. Prerequisites to success. Virtually any interaction from the remaining realms of relationship—conflict resolution, intimacy, parenting, family, money, world view, special interests—depend on your comprehension of these first five.

So right here we have the opportunity to self-assess.

How do you rate yourself in each of those behavioral realms (safety, authenticity, inner demons, tone, and love language)? How is your partner doing with them?

Perhaps there is a conversation to be had. Acknowledgement, confession, forgiveness, commitment. All of them, simply through recognition of what's working and what's not, and then reconciling any difference in perception between you and your partner, can take your relationship forward significantly, almost immediately.

It would be terrific if bliss were that simple.

Bliss in five parts... where do we sign up for *that*?

But it isn't that easy. You can get along with your dentist, but unless you are married to one, bliss is rarely a part of that relationship. Let us hope. Because you don't argue with your dentist, and you aren't—in a perfect world—intimate with her/him, either.

And therein resides one of the traps: if your relationship has descended to such a level—your experience with your partner is more like that of an associate, a friend, or even a brother or sister—then your pursuit of bliss is on hold.

Because what's next—the realms of conflict resolution, then sex and intimacy—is where bliss can manifest. Or, just as quickly where it disintegrates. Recognize this and you will have a head start on building a better life.

If bliss is truly your goal, good isn't good enough where conflict resolution and intimacy are concerned. You need to aim high within these realms, if nothing else than because of the risk involved. There is as much downside as there is upside potential awaiting in both facets of your interactions, and you'll need to master them in order for bliss—the real thing, the attainable kind, rather than some Danielle Steele version of it—to become a viable destination for the two of you.

The wording there is critical: *for the two of you.*

Think about it. Go over your past, and consider the primary relationships of everyone you have known or currently interact with. Who is truly happy, and who isn't?

Chances are you'll easily notice when conflict resolution is an issue. And chances are you'll have no clue whatsoever—at least where others are concerned—how intimacy either fuels or flattens a relationship. Because unlike conflict, where people tend to be open with their friends about what's not working, people clam up about their sex life in either direction, good or bad.

But you know how it is working in your relationship. Intimacy resides on a continuum: on one end is complete, stone cold dysfunction and distance; on the other is absolute, transparent unity and seamless integration.

The latter, even without consideration of all the other realms, becomes its own sort of bliss over time. Do you have this in your primary relationship? If so, how did you get there? If you've been together for more than a few years, probably not on autopilot. If not, where did things begin to taper off, perhaps until numbness set in? And why have you accepted it? Too much work? Too scary? No hope of fixing it? No longer interested in fixing it?

An open and courageous conversation can work wonders. Land where you will, but if you want a better life together, ignoring your issues is the worst possible choice you can make.

Bliss demands more from us than merely getting along.

Bliss is a house built on a foundation of genuine friendship, commitment, sacrifice and passion. It is nailed together with respect, and weathers the storms of life with forgiveness and a constant effort to live as the best version of yourself. For yourself and, just as much, for your partner.

This little list—respect, commitment, sacrifice, joy, passion, hope—becomes a pop quiz inventory you can take right now, as you read this. Any single omission or weakness can make the house come tumbling down.

True bliss has identified your B.S. and shown it the door. Or at least, remains in a constant state of mediation with it.

The secret weapon of conflict resolution.

In a full circle, paradoxical sort of way, intimacy is the key to conflict resolution. Because it requires an in-depth knowledge about your partner and yourself, with an awareness of when and how you may become your own worst enemy in moments of stress.

If a couple bickers, then their fights become an extension of that bickering. The snarky nit-picky parade of barbs creates the framework from within which they argue. Now consider a couple that is loving and fun and respectful as the baseline state. When they fight, that warmth still applies, completely changing the ways and means of any disagreement. They are quick to seek resolution, rather than an opening to deliver another blow.

If you can objectively step outside your relationship and look back into it with a therapist's sensibilities, you will see that any lack of or crack in the intimacy between you explains why you are less than completely happy. Because when intimacy wanes, you are to some extent alone, even within your relationship.

When that is the case, conflict resolution is an even bigger part of the equation.

Painless conflict resolution is intimacy-dependent.

Conflict within a relationship is inevitable. And thus, a healthy and productive approach and practice relative to conflict resolution is required if, much like fire, it is to be contained.

If truly you desire to make better choices when the heat turns up, you must become self-aware. You must learn to live in the pause and leave your negative energy in the locker room before you take the field. If your arguments are frequent and toxic, have a neutral conversation when things cool off about how you argue. Like an athlete who trains hard in practice when no fans are watching. Train for this together. Make rules about how you fight, and commit to them. It isn't about assigning blame or coaching your partner, but rather the first step is to acknowledge where you are in this regard.

When one of you loses it.

One of the most common pitfalls and challenges in relationships, even the good ones, is that one or both of the parties forgets that poor, unhealthy conflict resolution skills can lead to ruin. They can inflict damage that cannot be undone, forgiven or forgotten.

If, when you argue, one of you regularly "loses their shit," as they say, it may be time to seek mediation and counseling. Because this is like bringing a gun to a chess match. Nobody ever won an argument by losing their shit, and the loser walks away with damage that cuts deeply and lingers long.

Live in the pause. Take a breath when you'd rather scream out. Use that moment to observe and empathize where your partner is at that same moment, and respond with love instead of aggression.

Real love isn't parked or put on hold when the heat turns up.

Keep this one truth front and center when you feel yourself submitting to anger and pressure, and you'll have the opportunity to *live in the pause*, which is among the most empowering conflict resolution advice ever uttered.

You can find love in times of tension.

To be completely right, and yet not clobber your partner with that truth, is a moment of love. Just as to be completely wrong, and to offer submission to that truth, is also a moment of love.

To love in that moment when love, not to mention being kind, is the furthest thing from your mind, is to be courageous and wise. Wise enough to harness the moment for productive good, rather than allow it to take a bite that leaves a scar. Once those hurtful words and actions are released, they can never be taken back. There are always consequences.

The problem in most relationships, even within the ones that work, is that conflict resolution manifests more frequently as a means of warfare than the outcomes of intimacy. Negative emotions and responses arrive already fully ignited and informed by some remnant of residual emotion—resentment, the perception of unfairness, lingering and unresolved anger, stubbornness, embarrassment—perhaps from the last time you argued, and the time before that.

The goal should be to not continue an argument, but to diffuse one.

Everybody gets one strike. Chances are you and your partner are long past that point, which means the count is full and the next pitch is everything. If you swing and miss—if you say or do the wrong thing, in the wrong way—you are out.

On the other hand, if you simply surrender to the moment, acknowledge your emotions and those of your partner, if you take a deep breath to live in the pause, to summon the courage to give this moment of love to your partner, in spite of your anger or pain...

... then, when you can truly function at this level of conflict resolution, your relationship will change. For the better. It will happen almost immediately. The tough moments will be lesser, and further apart. The consequences of them will be diminished. What used to be arguments will evolve—devolve, if you will—into serious conversations, debates and negotiation, with both of you seeking the same goal.

Which is no longer to win, or to be right... but rather, to be loving.

My wife and I constantly wrestle with this.

We are very normal in this regard. We all wrestle with conflict resolution. It is the most challenging aspect of being in a relationship.

We agree on one thing. We acknowledge one scary truth between us, no matter what the issue-of-the-moment might be, and it's not good: we end up arguing about *how we argue* much more often, and to a much greater degree, than we differ about the issue itself. Which in retrospect are more triggers than something worthy of argument. With clearer heads they almost always flexible or negotiable, neither of which describes us in those initial moments of reactivity.

One of us raises a voice, or says something insensitive... and there it is. The issue falls away in favor of hurt feelings. Avoiding this paradox is about holding the offender accountable to our agreement to *not go there*.

Later, when cooler heads prevail, we talk about it and offer equal measures of vulnerability, apology and true conciliation. And in doing so we become even closer than before, with a renewed commitment to not allow ourselves to descend to those dark places again.

We got to this place because we had to.

We have polar opposite conflict resolution preferences. She is quick with a cutting word. I am quick to over-react. And then it's on. A side show of ridiculous irrelevance.

We also differ on how an argument should end.

For me, when something rings my emotional bell—anger or pain, it doesn't matter—I want to completely bang through to the conclusion of the issue. Nobody gets to the leave the room until both sides have aired, until any lingering hostility or resentment or inappropriate words or attitudes have been calmed, acknowledged and resolved. I detest unfairness, and being cruel is as unfair as walking out of the room.

Much easier said than done, by the way. But this is my goal.

My wife, on the other hand, wants to leave the room—sometimes storming out of it—until she has cooled off. "Just leave me alone" is her code to back off. Once the smoke clears she is as reasonable as I know she can be, calmly negotiating the issue at hand and apologizing for any harshness that wasn't productive. But in the ring, she's blind to whatever reason I'm trying to sell. Listening to me is the last thing she wants to do, no matter who crossed the line.

Both of us, in quieter moments, totally understand the preference of the other. In a twisted way it's a sort of love language. And yet, in those moments, both of us stick to our guns, which means she's trying to walk away while I'm standing in the doorway pleading my case. The discussion becomes a power struggle, riddled with a paradox of who-loves-who-more to decide which mode will rule the day.

I rarely win power struggles with my wife.

I'm betting this may sound familiar to you.

Thankfully this doesn't happen all that often, due in no small part to the calm and loving discussions we've had about this over the years, almost always after the emotions of disagreement have evened out.

So seldom, in fact, that it makes it easier than ever before to live in the pause when something rears its angry head. In that moment, because of our new agreement, it's easier to let it slide. To give the safe space to be less than emotionally perfect.

When it comes to conflict resolution and the discovery of what works and what doesn't, success almost always breeds success.

It is the reverse of that circle—a truly vicious circle when a couple can't summon the self-awareness and loving tonality required to argue successfully—that can smother the affection and tenor between you faster than anything going wrong within the other realms of relationship.

All of them are tested, or broken, by the realm of conflict resolution.

Here's the bottom line truth about conflict resolution: B.S.—yours, or your partner's—is always counter-productive. Even the slightest scent of it in your tone or behavior gets in the way of resolution, and makes understanding, compromise and forgiveness that much harder to achieve.

If you pout and give the silent treatment when you get mad… that's bullshit. You will pay consequences for it down the road.

If you say things that are unreasonably harsh and intended only to wound… that's bullshit. Those consequences will come back to you with a multiplier.

If you scheme revenge as a consequence of your unaddressed resentment… that's bullshit. You are truly at war in such a case, and in war everybody loses.

If you triangulate, or simply manipulate the truth to gain an upper hand, that's bullshit. This brands you going forward, in a way that makes it that much tougher to solve the problem. You're fighting unfairly, and this can cost you everything.

If you are condescending, cruel, manipulative, unreasonable, a conveyor of half-truths and selective memory, if you click into old tapes that have never worked but somehow summon your excuses or allow you to hide from yourself and your culpabilities... this is true bullshit.

In general... if you are an asshole, or a complete bitch, or even an incomplete bitch, who views and exists in the world through that filter (which is most often a perception on the part of everybody but you), then almost certainly your relationship will suffer for it. Suffer greatly, in fact. And you'll have a great defense ready, one that attempts to put all the blame on your partner, and/or relies on that old truism spoken only by idiots: *I'll never change, I am who I am.*

The truth in this regard is hard to hear and even harder to apply toward actually evolving toward a better version of yourself. Even then, though, tough as it may be, self-awareness is required. Especially if these tough-talk adjectives—asshole and bitch, and all the synonyms for it—happen to apply.

And if you cling to your B.S., it will, in large part, at the end of the day, be your fault.

The only thing that works within the realm of conflict resolution is authenticity (because bullshit is always a cover for something else), governed by love, delivered with the courage to handle the truth with kid glove skill that intends to heal, not punish. All approached with respect to an agreement about how you argue. The kind of stress and conflict born of the same kind of anger a healthy parent uses to address a misbehaving child: unconditional, loving, tough, courageous, forward-thinking, with an agenda of serving the child and your relationship, rather than giving voice and credence to your outrage, righteousness or indignation.

Or more simply, your bullshit.

The sweet spot of conflict resolution.

Rather than exclusively noticing and responding to how the other person is being within the moment/s of conflict, a better version of ourselves would notice how we—you—are being. How you are acting, what you are saying, doing, thinking, considering, remembering, or intending in those stressful moments.

We all know couples who have ended their relationship.

Statistics tell us that more than half of anyone reading this belongs to that club. By now all parties have made up a story—their own version of the truth behind the split—which remain unassailable… until those things come back to haunt them in their next relationship.

Hopefully they have—you have—learned something from the experience.

Of course, many variables contribute to tension between two people who love each other. Alcohol, to begin with, is the great disabler of conflict resolution, because it becomes a means of hiding, and thus a rationalization of cowardice and fear. Alcohol facilitates inauthenticity. But there are also side roads that allow us to be something less than our best selves. Major transgressions and the roads that lead to them—adultery, affairs of the heart, physical abuse, emotional coldness and cruelty, lying, deception, hypocrisy, drugs, illegal activity, resource-draining vices, pornography, family issues, zealotry—are usually bigger and more complex than couples themselves can address, and thus themselves evolve at a rate that smothers underlying best intentions or an initial willingness to work it out.

Once again counseling surfaces as your best option.

But sometimes not even the best therapy cannot summon the awareness and vulnerability that leads to change. Therapy is the real-life example of the old saying: when the student is ready the teacher will come. Too often the students can't handle the truth.

When much is required of us to make it work, for some it is easier to remain weak. To acknowledge being broken. To be unwilling to hear it, and just as unwilling to change.

Back in a prior life, I knew a couple who tried counseling and it didn't work. Someone forget to tell the husband that a) it wasn't going to be easy, and b) you just might have to look in a mirror during the process.

When he was a no-show for the second and third appointments, the therapist told the wife—who was sitting there alone at the time—there was nothing that could be done. That in effect she had two choices: live with this can't-be-wrong guy and the dysfunction defined by those traits, or make a change in her life. Which requires a different kind of courage.

Cut to a year later, and they were divorced. Happily so for her, not so happily for him. And yet, as he was complaining about what a cruel bitch his wife turned out to be, he was the guy who pulled the no-show, because he had too little self-awareness to visualize the consequences that lay ahead. The choice before him, as well as his wife and the therapist who were rooting for him, were clear to everyone but him. Yet he chose weakness, an easier low-road path that assumed his wife didn't have the guts to love herself enough to do what needed to be done.

Never underestimate the will of a woman who has snapped. I've lost touch, but I'm hoping she is happy, and that he has grown a pair so that he might end up that way, too.

And never misjudge the utter cluelessness of a man who can't sense the strength of a wife who has discovered her own greatness, if through nothing else than the realization that she is being short-changed in her relationship.

There are always consequences.

When *who you are* is the problem—when you are defined by your bullshit—then the work shifts to a process that relies heavily on that mirror so many are afraid to look into.

Bullshit can be survived. But only in the presence of an emerging self-awareness, within a relationship it hasn't already ruined beyond repair.

The goal is to use your love and your commitment to it as a buffer against the emotional strain of arguing. That love fuels you with the courage, strength and wisdom to conduct your confrontations, disagreements, disappointments and need to be heard with maturity, empathy and compassion. For yourself, for your partner, and for your relationship.

We need to love our partners in those moments when it is most challenging to do so. Not just as an acknowledgment of the big picture, but as the framing of what you say and how you behave when the pressure is on and the mirror stands before you.

Do that, and everything will change.

7. The Realm of Romance, Sex and Intimacy

For those who have thumbed through the table of contents and arrived here as your point of engagement with this book—ask yourself why—you should know two things. First, you may have missed the necessary context that informs this discussion. Or, secondly, if you're hoping for some graphic stuff... not gonna happen.

This chapter isn't about how to make love. Rather, this is about *why* to make love, and then, how to expand the definition of making love to embrace the entire potential of your experience of each other.

The word for that is *intimacy*.

If sex and romance aren't contributing to a bonding, memorable level of experience, something that dwells in your mind long after the candles have been extinguished—because you do make love to candlelight, right?—welcome to living with someone who seems more like a sibling than a lover. You may quietly grieve the loss of your lover. You may have even rationalized and accepted it as the perfectly normal course of growing old together.

But here is amazing, perhaps even disturbing news. Disturbing, that is, if you're not willing to put yourself out there in this regard.

Familiarity can actually become the spice of your love life, not the death of it. Understanding how to do this is the key to returning to the sexual bliss you once knew and had resigned to memory. But you may have to make some changes and accommodations to get there.

Maybe the frequency of your lovemaking has diminished.

Maybe it is non-existent, it's too much trouble these days.

Or maybe your head just isn't in the game. Some would claim that as you make love later in life, you may find yourself imagining (sublimating) someone else's face and body for that of your partner. I'm not here to judge or suggest what is proper, or not, but I will say this: in that case something has been lost. Unless this is part of fantasy roleplaying or simply acknowledgment between you. Matthew McCounaghey and Kate Beckensale have no idea how many heads and imaginary beds they've been in, in this regard. I say have at it, if this becomes the dirty little secret between you.

It didn't used to be that way. At least let us hope. With regard to the pursuit of bliss going forward, the goal is to become the object of your partner's deepest desires and fantasies, which is a massive challenge in relationships that have descended into pattern, cold comfort and laziness.

If your sex life isn't what it used to be, or what you wanted it to be at this point in your life—or if you're perfectly okay with both of those—you aren't alone. A vast majority of couples who have been together for many years, while assuring each other they are still very much in love, are likely no longer in *lust*. Many have stopped altogether. They rationalize this as normal, and they defensively ask, what's the point?

The point is your level of complete happiness. Nothing less than that.

Bliss is not normal.

But that question—*what's the point?*—is normal. It's how one responds to it that either empowers or disenfranchises your quest for bliss.

To attain some measure of complete fulfillment, to even legitimately claim the desire to seek it, requires that you take extraordinary, courageous and visionary measures. Many of which might test who you are, both as a person and as a couple.

Yes, it may be uncomfortable. Discomfort makes it easy to simply choose out, to accept a tepid status quo, rather than take any risks or make authentic effort.

We always have a choice in these matters.

If you are less than happy in this realm, intimacy is likely the very thing that has diminished between you, or at least changed into something you don't understand or recognize. When that happens it's usually more visible—as in, lacking—in the bedroom than anywhere else. And thus, it is the obvious starting place to begin the resurrection of desire.

This goes both ways: your sex is compromised because of a lack of intimacy, or intimacy is compromised because of a lack of sex. Both can be true at the same time, creating a vicious circle surrounding a void.

If you are too far down a rabbit hole, you have to do some digging before you can again see a bright horizon. Try to isolate the reasoning behind the chilly decline, and work from that point forward. What's the issue that causes this anxiety to surface? Fear of failure? Fear of acknowledging the truth, because the truth isn't something you completely understand, and it only points to the unavoidable fact that your youth is behind you?

Fear of looking silly in that fireman outfit she tells you she fantasizes about?

I know married couples who absolutely cannot maintain eye contact with their partner when they are anywhere near an intimate moment. Maybe—perhaps from Day One—one of them has insisted that the lights stay off.

In one workshop we took together, couples were asked to sit in silence and simply stare into each other's eyes for ten minutes. An eternity of inescapable intimacy, with nothing but the sound of your own thoughts thundering in your consciousness. Some couldn't do it, claiming it was silly. Others wept. A few left the room. And a few recognized truths that needed this contrivance to separate themselves from the distracting buzz of backstory and real life clutter.

If that level of intimacy makes you squirm, then you are down that rabbit hole. You need to fix your intimacy problem before you can fix your sex problem. The reverse approach won't go as well. I highly recommend you find professional help if this is your life.

By the way, intimacy workshops are out there. Find one, step out of your cynical, fearful skin and give it a go. The upside stakes should out-weigh your hesitance.

If you're still young and hormonally-engaged in this regard, maybe the notion of continuing to grow connects to the loss of the complete control you take for granted, and perhaps desperately need or cling to. Maybe it tests your boundaries in ways you aren't comfortable considering.

If you're older and hormones are the issue, the real question becomes your partner's level of satisfaction with this new status quo. If you're not on the same page, there are medicines and treatments beyond a little blue pill that can make you sexually young again.

In other words, you don't really have a valid excuse for accepting sexual decline.

I know of one couple that were married for a decade who never saw each other naked. True story. Never discussed it, either, which was every bit as much the problem. Even during the divorce, this never surfaced with lawyers in the room, any more than it did in the silence of the car on the way home from that final counseling session.

Think about it—they're married, and she never once saw her husband naked. Imagine the dysfunction elsewhere in that house.

I know another couple in which the woman confessed her frustration and lack of desire to a friend, someone who had been working on that very problem with her own husband. The friend confessed that her husband had a fantasy that for years she had ignored—she thought it was silly—but in response to their desire to spice things up he brought it up again. It involved wearing a certain thing to bed. Nothing all that weird, actually, something you might more likely wear to the mall on a rainy day.

So the first woman, the one hearing her friend rave about the wondrous result of this experimentation, decided to try it. Went to that mall, bought that same fetishized item, and surprised her husband that night with two things that were completely new to them: leaving the light on so he could see her, and then showing him a side of herself, a bold and dominating side that was wearing this "thing" that neither of them had ever considered in a sexual way.

When they were done she asked for feedback. Precisely what should have happened. He told her it was the most amazing thing he had ever experienced, the most exciting night of his life. And that she was never to do anything like that again.

DGD—Dumb Guy Disease—right there.

But it worked for her. It awakened something, a new path of potential and a new window into her deepest desires. His feedback worked, too, because it highlighted a truth she had suspected, but was now confirmed: her husband was F.U.B.A.R. in the head. Who would shut down something that had resulted in "the most amazing thing he had ever experienced?"

Someone who can't handle intimacy, that's who.

Cutting to the end—they were divorced shortly after. Certainly not solely because of what she wore and how it scared the testosterone out of him, but because they could no longer hide from his intimacy issues. He had outed himself in this regard. His unwillingness to step into something that required courage and the letting go of some very old inner demons caused the fallout, not the fetish.

Imagine if it had worked. Imagine the experiences they might have created together.

Once you see it, once you taste it, you cannot un-see it. Bear that in mind. It's why both of you need to be on the same page, or at least work to define that page in a way that works for you both.

Fear of intimacy. It's a deal killer. It's a bliss killer. Exploring it won't kill your relationship, but it might expose it and bring you to a crossroads. What you choose from there... that's on you.

The road to bliss has two lanes.

One coming, the other going.

Begin the process by doing the best job you can of owning up to where you are, what you want, and what about it stirs your anxieties. Discuss this with your partner, who—trust me on this—will be more than open and compassionate, because unless he/she is the guy from the previous example, in which case you're not gonna light the fire again anyway, the very fact of this surfacing is a sign of hope. And hope is what the partners of those who fear intimacy crave most.

The death of intimacy is the death of hope.

Sometimes couples get together because they actually share a fear of intimacy. They found someone who is just the same, someone that allows them to foster a co-dependence on the fear of intimacy. At first this becomes their common bond, they both prefer the lights be kept off. Anything beyond bowling and Friday night tequila shots together is more intimacy than they can handle, or would choose for reasons that connect back to old tapes they aren't open to examining.

I know another couple who began their life together like forbidden lovers united after decades of forced celibacy. Just out of prior marriages gone south, they banged each other into literal physical therapy and loved every bump and grind along the way.

Until they didn't. Until life got in the way. Health issues, family issues, money issues, and challenges surfacing from any of those previous realms you can no longer claim you don't recognize. A decade of chilly distance gradually commenced, so insidiously subtle that in any given moment they couldn't recognize the slippery slope they were descending. Resentment and a perfectly logical slide into a constant state of verbal joust ensued, and any hope of returning to that raging honeymoon energy became a silly extension of delusion. It simply never came up. They were too busy being miserable, too busy being busy to fess up to these truths, which everyone around them had no trouble identifying.

Until something snapped. Until those inner voices demanded to be heard. And when they spoke up, the other listened. The confession, the pain, the hope... all of it came from both sides, crashing in the air between them like simultaneously-launched ballistic missiles of emotion colliding over the ocean that had formed between their dreams and their emptying souls.

What remained, in spite of it all, was the love. This is not always the case, but the journey demands that you test these waters. Love was what fueled their courage to not hold back once this conversation began. The courage to listen. To embrace the other's experience and own their own role in it. To look each other in the eye and admit that time was growing short. That time itself was the one thing they had absolutely no control over. The rest of it... they could change.

They could *choose*.

I can't get too far into this without telling my own story in this regard.

Just today, as I wrote this, my wife came into my office and asked what I was working on. She knew it was this book, so the question required no more specificity. She wanted to know what section of the book I was writing.

I told her it was the chapter on romance, sex and intimacy.

She smiled, came close, kissed me on the top of my head as I sat before the computer screen, putting hands on both of my shoulders. "Well, that's certainly something you know a lot about, isn't it."

It was the *way* she said it. The way she touched me. Part of our own code, our dirty little secret. It spoke volumes. It screamed what was obvious: we remain *together*. We are intimate, even when we're not.

A dirty little secret shared with the love of your life becomes an aphrodisiac. A powerful key to bliss. Of course, many other things need to connect and click and resolve and refresh for this to remain vital, but those, too, stay enriched and empowered by what we share and have committed to.

This is the dance of love, millennia old and unchanged, other than the obsolete roles of head caveman and she who cleans the fish.

Find yourselves again. Resurrect, or even more empowering, discover something to share that becomes a delicious point of reference. Trust me when I say, the things you did and the way you did them when you were young probably no longer shock and amaze and brand themselves into your personal scrapbook of memories, locked in a private place in your head. Rather, you may need to try out some new moves, let go of some old stuff and trust in the process.

Set your fantasies loose. Tell your partner what you truly desire. You might be surprised at what happens when you embrace the ridiculous with complete and utter sincerity.

But what about *romance*?

Let me make this easier, shorter and sweeter than you might think.

Romance is the essence of that new, more intimate deal between you. Whatever it is you have created together. The simple act of living into this fresh realm of authentic safety, filled with a tone of love instead of the scent of B.S.-infused old tapes will lead to a flavor of romance of your own creation, totally unique to the two of you.

Like sex itself, romance is yours to define and put into practice. Doesn't matter what it is, whether it's out of a Nora Roberts novel or an A. N. Roquelaure trilogy. You get to say, you get to choose.

They call it a love *affair* for good reason.

The goal for those who seek bliss can be, almost literally, to have an affair with your significant other, and to conduct yourselves with the same level of passion and anticipatory focus as you would if your life was a movie and the two of you were living a raging love story in a Nicholas Sparks novel. Or even better, a dark erotic thriller.

Which—and this is both telling and wise—when taken literally, lends a sense of the naughty within how the two of you relate. No one else will understand, but the two of you will. It is the wise lover who understands when and how to incorporate the forbidden into a relationship. How to find, nurture and disappear into a healing, bonding, dirty little secret between you.

Wrestling with the demons of contradiction.

Some people claim that the tension—the very thing that, in those tense moments, keeps them from bliss—can actually fuel their lovemaking with passion. That make-up sex is the best sex.

In the short-term, perhaps. Maybe once in a while. But when conflict and the need for resolution become an on-going issue, a bone of contention over time (absolutely no pun intended), a price is paid relative to the intimacy between the two parties.

You can only argue for so long without attaining resolution before the other person *becomes* the issue. When that happens, a huge asterisk descends on everything that goes down (also no pun intended) between you.

Do what you want.

Live your dream. Do whatever your partner wants. And if that challenges you, negotiate the middle ground and try to meet there, or at least be willing to try life at either end of the scale.

The notion that women want soft gooey romance spiced with cheesy erotic dialogue, and men want urgent satisfaction in complete silence, preferably with big boobs… that's a myth. An easy rationalization of the frustrated and unenlightened, a way to hide behind your gender.

We have been sociologically and parentally programmed to buy into those rationalizations of what constitutes manliness and femininity, often to the exclusion or at least the detriment of a fuller scope of possibility.

If your partner's definition of masculinity and femininity put boundaries on what you desire from each other, then this becomes part of the problem. Trust me, women want a good romp in the jungle as much as men do. Men also want to be touched. Needed. To be held afterward. Especially in a committed relationship.

It's all in the mind. It always has been—just as the upside potential also will spring from the mind—beginning with those archetypes we inherited from our parents. But we have the power to control our minds and shift those paradigms. We have the power to choose.

These are precisely the roles you need to throw out the window as you seek to reinvent yourselves sexually, romantically, and intimately. The key is to talk about it, openly and frequently. Be as open as you are courageous. Suggest the outrageous. Make it safe for your partner to take a risk and be vulnerable.

Of course, I don't advocate that the "outrageous" include sexual activity outside of the bonds of a committed relationship. Not because I'm a prude or because I judge it harshly—not my place here, other than reminding you that it may violate the commitments you have made—but because doing so will become an inevitable source of resentment and toxicity in a relationship.

Intimacy resides in the mind

Sex and intimacy—when one works, the other is empowered until there comes a point at which any divisiveness begins to melt away. Intimacy is desire colliding with a reality made contextual through actions and words, through intention and perception.

The great liberator, the secret of great lovers and legendary romance, is to make love to your partner's *mind*, as much as embracing the flesh.

Anticipation is the spice of passion.

To not talk about it is to embrace old fears and laziness. To not talk about it is to forego one of the most titillating opportunities inherent to living together in love. Words are the secret sauce of pleasure. Great lovers get this. They understand that virtually and literally narrating the story you are crafting together is the foreplay of the mind. Which is the most sensitive and responsive sexual organ in the human body, male or female.

As we grow older together, it is inevitable that spontaneous sex becomes less likely and perhaps less rewarding.

But we don't need to accept that as inevitable. There are work-arounds, and the opportunity to grow your sexual life together rather than submit it to the erosion of time.

In researching this book, I met a couple who have what they call Date Nights on a regular—and, because they are not spring chickens—age-appropriate basis. They didn't invent the term, but they may have come close to reinventing it.

They were eager to talk about it on an assurance of anonymity, because they didn't want their friends to know.

For them, Date Night has completely replaced any form of spontaneous sex. It requires preparation and mid-course adjustments that take the spontaneity out of things. They assure that what they practice, relative to a sex life, is orders of magnitude more fun and rewarding than the more common, and their former, *roll-over-I-want-you* type of lovemaking.

A few days before the big evening, which has been set aside for a week or so, they share a bottle of wine and talk about—hint at, toy and flirt with—what might happen. She knows how to get into his head with specificity, and he knows how to lead her there. The conversation doesn't become a script, it becomes its own sexual encounter, even though the only exchange of physicality is via the eyes, body language and words.

For them, Date Night isn't about going out, it is about staying in.

A few days later, on the actual Date Night, they share another glass of wine before the husband leaves the house for about two hours.

Yes, your read that right. There are no rules and no expectations when it comes to sexuality, we all get to make it all up as we go along. And this is what they do.

His wife uses that time to luxuriate in her femininity as she prepares for her lover to return, trying on this and that, playing with the possibilities. This not only gets her in the mood—which began a few days earlier with that first teasing glass of wine—it hits the pause button on real life and allows her to step into an alternate state of being, a world in which only the two of them exist, the boundaries and expectations for which are of their own creation.

There is no over-stating how powerful this is within the bigger picture of their lives. They relive it over the ensuing days and weeks with something as little as a knowing glance, a double-entendre word or two, or an embrace that is a bit tighter than it normally would be. In essence, in the autumn of their lives, they are lovers again.

Imagine your dreams coming true.

If you can wrap your head around the possibilities, you can change your life going forward, and on all levels. You can refuel, recharge and begin anew on a journey of sexual awakening and exploration unlike anything you'd dare share with even your closest friends.

Choose intimacy. Let go of what limits you, and be open to what may actually define you. Commit to making your partner the happiest, most fulfilled person on the planet by tapping into that secret place in her/his mind, to which you are now eagerly admitted.

Let this be either the cause or effect of falling in love again. Both are available when you strip away all the distractions and baloney that conspires to take you down, or at least put you to sleep.

8. The Realm of the Everyday

All this, and yet there is more to it.

The previous behavioral realms of relationship—safety, authenticity, inner demons, tone, love language, which are implemented via conflict resolution and intimacy—pretty much encapsulate how we live into a host of other everyday challenges and situations. These become the armor we wear into the arena to confront a plethora of outside states and situations, pressures, influences and problems as they collide with interior motivations, values, priorities, moods and backstories.

The result becomes a complex emotional matrix that frames our responses to them. It is no wonder so many couples struggle, because the number of influences and options within that matrix boggle the mind. Autopilot stands no chance.

The key is to be aware that you do have a choice about how you respond. The poster child of victim rationalization—"well *excuse me* for being human in the face of a real problem"—doesn't cut it when the tools are at your fingertips.

There is no excuse, ever—even if you're in the right, if you're angry or if you're hurting—for being an insensitive ass or bully that makes your partner feel unsafe. That is simply your inner childhood spoiled brat acting out in a way that is unkind, unfair or unreasonable.

The goal is to eventually make more productive and courageous choices a reflex. To make them your first choices. Until then, we need to rely on our own awareness—even above our instincts, at least until they become sound—so that we may choose wisely when old tapes and fresh challenges call our name.

Reinventing ourselves in this regard, or at least summoning the best version of ourselves, is no small task. Those old tapes are loud. Autopilot is seductive because it feels so natural and easy. What has become habit—because there haven't been sufficient consequences to motivate change—will resist the new you and the new normal you seek to establish.

Change is monumentally hard for most human beings.

Those who are lazy, weak, selfish, narcissistic, or have a sensitivity chip missing will struggle with the prospect of change. They'll rationalize and defend their immovable positions with great passion. "Screw this, and screw you," is the common denominator essence of their response.

Begin the process with *you*.

In considering an upgrade in our primary relationship, there are two questions we should pose to the mirror on a regular basis: which of those broken inclinations are you guilty of, and what are the insidious long-term consequences that have come of it?

Along with this one: *doesn't my partner deserve better?*

Your answer may indeed be *no*. Which, in that case, becomes the starting point for the journey toward the changes that you need to create between you.

Sure, we'll all have bad days and weak moments. Let us never forget that these realms—both behavioral and from the everyday—are a normal part of the process of living together.

191

With a healthy responsive *new normal* in play, challenges can actually be harnessed as opportunities to grow. To sharpen awareness. To be held accountable. To protect and to serve, which is the core of your commitment to be your best self and to love without hesitance, condition, agenda or restriction.

Imagine your response if your partner, formerly prone to over-reaction and lashing out, suddenly responded to a tough problem with calm resolve, honesty, and a willingness to meet you in the middle? You would be, perhaps quietly, ecstatic.

You should *be* that partner. Be the first one in.

When you get to that point, you will witness the absolute miracle that awaits when your bond, cemented by this commitment and evolved into a more loving place, is stronger than the shifting tides of life that promise to test it. It may take time, but if your partner is worth the work, you will absolutely get there.

Or, you may finally realize that your partner isn't worth the work. In which case you arrive at a crossroads in your life: to settle, to begin the hard work of change, or to make another choice.

The daily challenges, met in context to our backstories, are where hidden triggers await. Where we will be confronted and stretched and tempted to resort to prior views and behaviors and thus, reverting back to responses and resentments we now understand may not work as we would intend or understand, or that just seem easier and natural in the moment.

Those easy choices are the enemy. Not your partner.

As we tick through these everyday challenges, keep the goal in mind.

Life isn't fair. And within that awaits a nasty little landmine of wisdom: while it may be true that you have a wealth of wonderful, loving feelings between you, it is the *negative* responses to challenge and conflict that will put your relationship at risk.

One impatient, harsh word or even a disapproving look can ruin an entire day. Or more. It may be a wound, with a scar forthcoming that quietly remains even after you have forgiven and believe it to be forgotten.

Emotional pain may be forgiven, but it is rarely forgotten.

With a new, more loving *normal* alive and well in your relationship, those moments are not only fewer, the consequences are minimized. When the overall tenor of your energy is loving and positive, you get more leeway, more rope.

The goal is not to be perfect.

It can't be. Because perfect is impossible.

Rather, the goal is to strive for it from an awareness of when and how you fall short. To temper anxiety, tension and pain with compassion, empathy and through living in the pause when temptation knocks. To seek to live into and from a place where a better response almost is always available. To recognize blame as something toxic, yet to accept it when warranted. To ask for and offer forgiveness. To work together on the commitments you share, to talk about these things often and deeply, holding each other accountable, when doing so feels like the last thing you'd choose because at the moment things are rough and emotions are raw. To foster intimacy that leads your partner to the attainment of her/his highest self and most deeply held needs, and delivers fulfillment and experience. Even when it stretches you.

To under no circumstances allow your partner to feel alone, unsafe, or unsure.

Never step over an opportunity to give something to your partner that takes you forward together. It is amazing how much healing power there can be in a loving touch, a warm glance, a soft tone. Even more so when the pressure is on.

As simple as that sounds, relationships that have built up a lot of negative energy and resentment will be hard-pressed to even consider these responses. Your lesser self believes that some form of justice or accounting is required before you can move into this more loving space. That you need to get some things off your chest before you can click into it.

If you recognize this to be the case for you, the best possible solutions are to: a) acknowledge it to your partner, and b) get some professional help to navigate the conversations you feel are necessary before you can assume the mantle of affectionate and intimate love.

Resentment, along with the loss of respect and hope, can be an insurmountable barrier to bliss, or even a simpler contentment. And yet, if you fail to recognize this and step into confrontation with it in tow, you become victim to it. Right or wrong won't matter.

Dead is dead, and you can be *dead right* in this equation.

Perception, Management and Disagreement

Consider how many arguments, or at least those dark moments during which one or both of you has been hurt, that you have had relative to family... parenting... money... career... friends... religion... politics... difference of opinion of what's true, what's best, where you should or should not go or what you should or shouldn't do... or simply your differing world views.

Maybe you were once on the same page, but have grown apart. Or maybe these differences are the consequences of other dysfunction, and you are using them as a means of expressing your frustration with who she/he is as a person, which is absolutely a ticket to counseling if that applies.

These are the big issues in your relationship. Even when they're not. That's the point, you see... to not allow the little things, the inevitable differences, to become big things by virtue of unhealthy, dysfunctional or simply asinine responses and behaviors.

Asinine behaviors beget consequences infused with, or eliciting, more asinine behaviors. This is true for both of you: when under stress or pressure, you are not licensed to be impatient or to lash out to your partner. Not because I say so, or any other advisor in this realm says so, but because of the natural phenomenon of consequences.

This vicious circle is common, and thus, the stuff of *normal*. But you have committed to live above the standards of normal in your pursuit of mutual fulfillment. These are the times when that commitment matters.

Too often any of these everyday domestic hotbeds of differing views can become seeds of resentment, resistance and even revenge, the latter undertaken in the slippery-slope name of fairness. For example—forgive the gender stereotypes here, feel free to swap out the pronouns as you please—she resents the fishing gear you just purchased on a credit card, after you made it clear that the new curtains she wants in the bedroom are too expensive. More than that fly rod, by the way.

But hey, life is for living, not for looking out through windows... right? And so, you disagree. You rationalize. You argue. And both of you *resent* it.

Resentment is like swallowing a bottle of weed killer. You wash it down with your self-righteousness. But it never leads to anything good. Never. It is toxic by its very nature. The only thing that it kills is the host itself, eating a hole in vital organs, one by one. It can kill you if not recognized and extracted.

Awareness is the antidote to emotional toxicity.

Because only then can you see the big picture, and your role within it. Anxiety and anger become goggles that block a view of the whole picture. If the anxiety of the moment is bigger than you are, work toward using a keener awareness to acknowledge it. It will almost always be more two-sided than you thought it was from behind those goggles.

Acknowledgement is the very thing that allows you open up a dialogue that can ultimately lead to ridding yourself of resentment and anxiety. Which you must if you are to clear the path toward bliss.

Such arguments are never about who is right or who is wrong. It is about who is reasonable and responsible, and who is, in a given moment, not. Who is trying to even the score or who simply forgot that there are two names on the utility bill. When you move into that frame of understanding, everything changes.

Sometimes you may need to agree to disagree. Sometimes you'll simply need to lose a few. And sometimes, if this doesn't get the best of you, you are awarded a win because of no other reason than your partner getting this, and loves you enough to give you what might otherwise be a draw.

When this give-and-take is dysfunctional, the same culprits are to blame: stubbornness, cluelessness, selfishness, defensiveness, old tapes and resentments, each of which is fertilized by lack of skill across all seven of the realms of relationship we have discussed.

And when you can navigate these waters smoothly, the same set of tools apply. The tools of mastering those previous seven behavioral realms of relationship: cultivating a safe place to be honest and open... being authentic in your words and actions... being less a taker and more a giver, more often... resolving differences that don't escalate because of inner demons or short-term memory... negotiating from the intention of partnership, intimacy and love, rather than holding your ground or keeping things even between you.

Awareness is the centerpiece of this skill set.

How aware are you of your own responses and how they are perceived? Are you coming from a place of enlightened love, or is emotion, autopilot and fear driving who you are when the dark moments rise up to challenge you?

What kind of man are you if you cannot, or refuse, to stand tall and wise in the face of challenge and temptation that can take you down? What kind of protector are you, how strong are you, if you can't stand up to your own weaknesses and beat them back, simply by making better choices about your responses to them?

What kind of woman are you if you defer to anything short of your own sense of self and virtue, especially with regard to the commitments you've made? And if you believe, perhaps rationalized by that self worth, that you adopt an aggressor role that is less than kind, less than loving, when you partner isn't the problem, but life itself is?

Of course, there may be genuinely unwinnable arguments to deal with. When a disagreement is unwinnable, a possible outcome short of negotiation and compromise is resentment. Which leads to resistance and even retaliation. Every argument becomes a rabbit hole that you have already been digging.

The goal isn't necessarily to agree. That's not realistic when there are underlying values and deeply held convictions fueling your positions. Some issues are too complex to reduce to right versus wrong. The goal is to create a loving framework for discussion and efforts at compromise and resolution relative to the issues.

My wife and I openly discuss our strengths and weaknesses all the time, especially in the context of stress. Not that we have these discussions in those moments. We don't. When the heat is on we try to manage old tapes to remain civil and productive. Then we dissect the hard conversations later, when the emotional tenor is completely different, and both us of are more open and vulnerable.

If you've never experienced this postmortem evaluation of how you did during the clash, you're missing something very special. This is when acknowledgement is easiest and most productive, and when negotiations and compromises can be sealed, literally with a kiss.

Issues of style.

You are an optimist, your partner is, in your opinion, consistently negative. You are a doer, your partner is a procrastinator. You are a thinker and a planer, your partner is spontaneous, a go-for-it type, who may or may not apologize later after the bottom falls out. You are loud and extroverted, your partner quiet and introspective.

On paper you shouldn't work.

You view the world through a different lens. Maybe you remember when that wasn't the case, and you long for those days. Something has changed. Or perhaps, over time, your love goggles have fogged.

Sometimes the very differences that attracted you to each other can become toxic. Time has changed your view and perhaps evolved the formerly fun and attractive into the boring and downright irritating. Your partner used to be the funniest person in the room, now he/she is just the most desperate for attention, at least in your eyes.

Over time, such opinions about your partner's style may become either cause or effect. Again, the point isn't so much about being right and successfully changing your partner—not a high-odds proposition, that—but rather, to become highly and keenly aware of the source of both the behavior you are noticing and your reactions to it. From that awareness you may find clarity, both in terms of understanding and reacting.

To react without understanding and empathy is to throw rocks. One rock begets the next, and soon they are flying in both directions.

The moment you are arguing about how you argue, the wise move is to shut it down. To simply shut up. Take a break, live in the pause until you see things more clearly. Or, if you can quickly shift into a healthier mode—and *only* then—focus on that particular dysfunction before doing anything else.

Later is by far the best time to talk about how you argue. It is the wise couple who can read the temperature clearly enough to know which to choose.

My wife is a fixer.

It is her natural inclination. She has learned that when I am stressed-out about something—because we have had more than a few postmortems on this issue—that instead of reciting a litany of options and solutions, most of which I'd already considered and therefore kicks me into a mode of impatience, the more productive style is to simply listen. To allow me to arrive at the place in the discussion where I let her know that I'm considering my options and am aware of the obvious. At that point I am no longer impatient with spontaneous suggestions, I welcome them.

Launching a discussion about concerns on these fronts will almost always feel like judgement or criticism, which may raise the hairs of defensiveness and triangulation. It is as critical that you understand this from the delivery side as it is from the receiving end of feedback.

My wife tells me that my silence works against me. I'm tall, I look more like an old ex-linebacker contemplating a comeback than I do a novelist. People make assumptions about me simply from the way I look and carry myself, which leads to certain perceptions that may push their own buttons and rile up a few inner demons. My stillness and my physical stature can confirm their fears, however unfounded.

To make matters worse, I'm naturally on the quiet side. I have no need to be the focus of attention in every room I'm in. Stillness is easily misinterpreted. I have to try harder than some, since to remain still is to solicit misperception, including one that colors me as disinterested. We discuss this often, because it comes up often. And always, I have to walk back a defensive response, when vulnerability is the higher choice. Because she's right. She's not seeking to bring me down, she's seeking to lift me to a better version of myself.

An effective tool to address style differences is to ask permission to be honest, ask if now is a good time for that, and if not, schedule one. Request that your partner, to whom you are about to deliver threatening feedback, remain open and vulnerable.

This is not the time to vent. To empty your frustrations. Rather, this is the time to set the stage for understanding and change, which depends on disabling defensiveness before it takes over.

If permission is authentically granted—you'll know if there is anything begrudging about your partner's opting in—that alone may diffuse any negative energy you might otherwise have spewed into the space between you. In that case you'll already be on a natural path toward achieving change and the growth you feel are called for.

There is much to negotiate.

The way you think, the way you live. The actions you take, the things you say. Every day brings the opportunity to rise and shine, or stumble and fall. Our best hope of becoming truly happy and fulfilled is to be positively perceived. To understand how we are contributing either to our successes or failures. How we are responding. Most importantly, the energy we put forth, and what it all means in the long run.

To survive, to reach bliss, requires patience.

To dodge the onslaught of threat, born of resentment, requires forgiveness.

To navigate the storms of the world, requires peace and grace.

To do the right things, requires strength and courage.

To know what those right things are, requires faith and awareness.

To maintain what you've created and move it forward requires growth. Growing together. And yet, standing apart, giving your partner the room to strive for things, and a safe space to fail.

When you sense the chemistry getting tepid or thin, embark upon a full court press toward injecting your relationship with the steroids that lead to bliss. Revisit your passion, your desire and your best self. Recite the attributes of winning at love: awareness, selflessness, proactivity, living in the pause, and creating an empowered new normal between you that results in positivity within those behavioral realms. Strive for safety, authenticity, the disenfranchisement of inner demons, a tone and language of love, an efficient and loving response to conflict, and a level of intimacy that the world cannot break and time cannot diminish.

These are all choices. After a while they can become default modes of being.

The trick, the key to everything in a relationship—because it becomes the consequence of everything—is to make it easy for your partner to see the best and highest choices in all these regards.

It won't be easy for either of you. But for it to work, it needs to begin with you.

The Everyday Playbook of Bliss

So here we are, you and me. You in your relationship, me in mine. Now what? If one million people read this—which is my hope—then there would be one million different combinations of, and reactions to, everything we've just covered.

As it should be. We're all different. We all need and want different things, in varying degrees and flavors. But I believe it's fair to say that in love, some things are non-negotiable: respect, kindness, support (which takes many different forms, including listening, tough-love, setting limits or sometimes just a shoulder to cry on), sharing, an environment of safety and a tonality of affection, and hope that it will all move forward and grow.

There would also be one million starting points that are unique to each couple, and that particular factor has yet to be addressed. Because it may actually frame who you are today, with the ghost of who you were whispering that whatever troubles your partnership may be your fault, at least partially.

Because you picked him or her, after all.

If the guy is a beast now, he may have been a beast in sheep's clothing when you got together. Maybe, in a sexual chemistry sort of way, that beast was what turned you on. Or, if she's a raving, unreasonable bitch these days, perhaps that woman was on her best behavior back in the day, and through the steam on your love goggles you didn't see it.

And now you're stuck with each other. What to do?

The principles that will serve you in this paradox are pretty basic. They also become windows into where and how the defining energy between you may have broken down.

So basic, that you may have shoved them to the side of your awareness.

First, be a good person. Because your partner is watching.

Be good to your partner. Put her/him first. Be a giver. Hold each other accountable. Master the realms of relationships we've just discussed. Don't be selfish and cold and distant. Watch your tone. Listen to, and care about, how you come off. Value her/his opinions and empathize with their fears. Give her/him space to be human, to make mistakes, because walking on egg shells isn't sustainable. Have some fun. Don't be an ass.

Don't keep score, because this isn't a game. When you see a foul, call it out, then work it out.

Don't ever allow your partner to disrespect you. Because respect is an essential component of bliss, or even a modicum of happiness. But within that, don't perceive your partner calling you out as disrespect. It's just the opposite. Notice and honor your partner's courage to hold you accountable.

Breakdowns may have crept into your life, insidiously, with varying degrees of intensity and frequency. Just when you think you can't take it anymore, the good-partner shows up, buying more time, quieting that old voice in your head. Injecting a little hope that this might become the norm, as it once was. Maybe something will change. Maybe we'll go back to who we were.

Maybe it isn't so bad, after all.

If anything close to any of that echoes in your head, then chances are you're not living in bliss. Limbo is more like it. Or hell itself. Such a realization doesn't make any of the challenges go away, per se, but rather, it may lead to a more loving platform for change.

And change always begins with you.

Love is like a spacesuit, it sustains life and shields you from a toxic, deadly atmosphere. Maybe all you need to do is plug a small leak. A leak that, over time, can kill you.

Most of all, you need to talk about it.

Frequently. Deeply. With empathy, patience, and even strategy that takes your partner's experience, fears and responses into account.

Turn off the television. Share how you feel and where you are on the path. Offer coaching and feedback, and ask for it in return. Avoid the hot buttons, but don't shy away from the truth of what you need and want. Be soft, but stay strong. Don't settle. Tell each other what you need, what you desire.

There is nothing wrong with defining a best-case scenario outcome for your relationship negotiations. Sell it. And then, when your partner grabs the microphone, be open. Really listen. Try to understand why it's not happening as planned. Why your partner might resist, resent or simply not understand. Be persistent and patient. Negotiate where you have to.

One step at a time is better than nothing. Put your foot down when you have to, as well… hopefully not anywhere near where the sun doesn't shine.

Your capacity for bliss, and that of your partner, is a key variable.

Are you asking the impossible? Can change really happen between you? These answers define your path to a significant degree.

We're on our own on that count. There isn't a book in print that shows us how to navigate our own relationship path with specificity, with our own unique backstories, emotions, and sense of fear.

We are left with principles, rather than specifics. It is our job to consider the variables we are dealing with in relation to those principles.

I've talked to people about this stuff, and sometimes all they can say is, "Yeah, I know," with a sad-sack tone of resignation. Because they're afraid to be authentic. Fearful of taking the risk that honesty and transparency requires. They may say they know, but they don't really know.

What they don't know, I believe, is what their partner is going to say or do when confronted with a new level of authenticity and courage.

My goal has been to give you two things: an awareness arising from greater clarity across a broad range of relationship forces and issues... and a tool chest for dealing with it. A means of creating change within yourself, which I hope you now realize is essential to launching down a path of healing, growth and the pursuit of something better.

Or maybe the need for change is more immediate. Maybe strong action is required. Once again I urge you—I beg you—to not go it alone if the courageous path looks like it may lead you off a cliff. Find the right counselor. Ask your friends, do some research. And when you get in front of that person, be abundantly clear and fair when you present your side and your hopes.

That line at which you settle is fuzzy.

It shifts and bends in ways you can't explain. But deep inside, you know the line is yours to define and negotiate.

The degree of difference between who you are now and who you were when you began isn't as simple as recognizing that your relationship has clicked into autopilot mode, or that the two of you, perhaps simply through inattentiveness, have allowed negative energy and harsh tonality to erode the dream you signed up for. Yeah, that's what happened. But the real question is... why? And what part of it did you create and/or contribute to? And are you willing to own it?

To some extent you stepped into your destiny by virtue of not only who you chose, but the criteria for that choice at the time.

Hopefully the love has grown, even if some of the realms within it need dusting off. That, too, is a matter of perception and degree. You've changed. Your partner has changed. What do we do with this new awareness, the evolved state of love—in either direction—that defines the relationship now?

If you had a do-over, would you make the same choice? That's a tough, telling, empowering question if you have the clarity and courage to address it. Your answer doesn't have to send you packing. But it might help you wrap your head around the process of change and growth before you. The point of taking that snapshot is to realize the nature of the choices you must make.

Because who *you* are is the only thing you can completely control.

The alternative is dark.

You knew that when you opened this book, and perhaps reading this far has shined a new light on what is working and what isn't. Why he might cheat on you. Why she might leave for a new life. What you contribute to that possibility, and how you might embark on a journey of healing, forgiveness and change. Now...

Allow me to be more specific.

To toss out some practices, choices, actions and attitudes that are more about fostering a positive climate of love and bliss between you, as opposed to simply applying them to the more challenging and darker moments when we are being tested, when it is harder to summon our best selves.

Here are some things you can actually do, on a daily basis, that will contribute toward a softer, more loving, more intimate connection between you.

Tell your partner you love her/him... every single day.

If that sounds unbearably awkward and cheesy, then you have a problem. And the problem might just be you.

Intimacy fuels primary relationships. If you struggle with it, the relationship pays a price. It is on you to change this.

I've asked couples how often they say "I love you" to each other. Sometimes the answer is... hardly ever. Or every few months, when we're drinking or having sex. Or on our anniversary, with a little peck of a kiss.

To me, this is unthinkable. I tell my wife that I love her several times a day. I layer it with compliments and admiration. I positively gush, and I mean every word of it. We are one of those couples that, even if you know us, can make you sick with the airborne affection between us. Not PA, just an obvious passion and respect for each other.

Most women want to be adored. Even if they are the toughest, most outspoken feminist icon of fierceness. With her partner, she wants to be worshipped.

But it doesn't stop there. This isn't about narcissism. They also want to be made to feel worthy, equal and intelligent—because they are—as well as desirable. They want to feel safe. Protected. They want to trust and respect their partner. They want to contribute. They want you to give them something to root for where you are concerned. Never assume they want to be their mother, who also desired to be adored.

Whatever the roles you've agreed upon within the relationship, women want to know that you appreciate who they are and what they contribute. As mothers and lovers and professionals, they want to know that you honor their work, their contribution, without compromise.

Men, your goal is to make her feel all of that, in abundance, without doubt, without gaps and with passion and hope taking you both forward.

Men want to feel strong and protective.

They want to provide. They want the chance to step into their masculinity, which has nothing at all do with hunting or fishing or cigars or fixing toilets or other prior-generation clichés. But it does have everything to do with creating solutions and protecting his partner, because that is his contribution, and he wants you to notice.

Women, let your man know how safe and protected you feel. How nice it is to know he can handle whatever life throws at you, and tell him that you noticed and it sort of turns you on.

For many women, testosterone remains their drug of choice. Manage it well and you'll reap a benefit some men take off the table by virtue of their own ignorance.

Dumb Guy Disease. Don't be *that* guy.

Don't cast your choices in concrete.

I'm not here to judge the roles you've assumed in your relationship. If those roles are traditional, perhaps those of your parents, that's absolutely a path to bliss if it is not a concession or an unreasonable expectation. It works when it is a choice on both your parts. Just make sure it isn't locked in, in such a way that it feels like a raw deal.

It's when one grows out of that choice—often because their partner begins to take it for granted, or assigns it to the will of God, or doesn't appreciate the other wanting to stretch her/his wings—and hasn't negotiated a new normal, that problems can arise. Because resentment is inevitable. And when resentment settles in, resistance and retaliation are never far behind.

Years pass. You grow. You need something new. You're bored and tired of what you've been doing. Parties within a healthy relationship don't seek to hold their partner back, they are all about the growth of their partner. They nurture it, they cheer it, they welcome it.

Consider, for example, the woman who has been making a home for her family, which was very much her choice. She'd held a variety of jobs, including those years as a homemaker and mother. Maybe she shelved a professional career to make that choice, to work at home as the caretaker and mother and provider of domestic basics and comfort. Then, years later, at some point she decides she wants to return to the workplace in a professional capacity, an idea which doesn't sit well with her very traditional husband. And so the veiled conversation begins, unspooling over time, neither side getting the approval they need.

Finally, when there is no more hiding from the real issue, her husband becomes authentic. Strategically so. A hail Mary. He tells her he doesn't want her to go back to the workplace—

maybe even forbids it—because she would end up leaving him.

Ah, a surprise ending there. How can she not calm his anxiety in this regard? How sweet, he loves her that much that he wants to hold her in virtual captivity, all to himself.

And thus, the stage is set for irony to manifest.

Of course, the next question is *why*? Imagine the toxicity that has led to this point. Notice how this last ditch explanation is at once a compliment and an admission—all very manipulative in nature and by intention—the latter being that he was the self-anointed King of their castle, that he had one-up on all the other guys out there, and if she began to walk among them she would discover his façade. That he's not the smartest, coolest guy out there after all.

My guess, though, is that in such a situation—which is everywhere out there—he fears she would discover her own greatness... which is precisely what happens almost every time.

Growing is essential. Growing together... is bliss.

Epilogue: that is precisely what happened. She discovered her own greatness, not because other men flocked to her (they did), but because it was there all along. Divorced followed within two years.

The take away: nurture your spouse's greatness and complete fulfillment, before she/he feels the need to seek it elsewhere.

Say the unexpected.

Your partner thinks they know you. Thing is, when there is nothing new to learn, boredom might be next.

The thrill of a new relationship is the discovery process, so why not give your long-term partner something new to discover about you? Look for an opening to say—or even do—the opposite of what your partner would expect, and do it from a positive intention. Then be prepared to talk about it later. Welcome discussion. Embrace it for the empowering elixir that it is.

Not a flowers kind of guy? Bring her flowers. Don't like movies? Take her to the next popular chick-flick. Don't dance? Enroll the two of you in a ballroom dance class. Has something been lingering on the family to-do list? Just do it.

The entire proposal of intimacy, of the launch of a new sexual adventure between you, is an example of how you can rock the world of your partner.

Assume a new role in the household. If the domestic work has been distributed unevenly, for whatever reason, even if it was once agreed to, off-load some of your partner's regular chores, and stick to it. Even doing this once in a while will earn significant points.

Make a new agreement between you. Based on who you are now, as individuals and as a couple. Anticipate what your partner needs, and make it happen. Show her or him that you've changed, and the direction of that change is a good thing for both of you.

If she/he wants change, make it happen.

These things add up. And over time, they can add up to bliss.

Tell your partner why you fell in love, unsolicited.

Just do it, out of the blue. Talk about the old days, when your blood ran hot and your any vision of the future had her/him in it. Narrate how that love has evolved to become stronger than ever.

You might be asked what your agenda is, and your answer is that it just popped into your head—that it pops into your head frequently—and you wanted to share your feelings. Don't use the past as a comparative criticism, but rather, as a return to the old magic. Let it sink in, don't expect anything back. Because it will come back to you, only later.

Not long ago I had the urge to do just this. A regular day, nothing prompting a sudden rush of emotion on my part. We call it a *love attack*, and we always tell the other when it happens.

On this day—and I wasn't making this up—I had been in the car alone and I began inventorying the myriad facets of my wife's personality. Not all of it was good, we'd had a particularly challenging morning, when we were once again bickering about how we argue rather than the issue itself, which had already been forgotten. I'd kidded that she has thirty-two personalities (coincidentally, early in our marriage there was a hit country song about just that, "Lucky 4 You," by SheDaisy... YouTube it, have a listen, it'll make you smile), and that I was madly in love with twenty-seven of them.

So later, sitting on the couch, I recalled the emotion of that little day- dream reverie, and decided to tell her about it. She clicked off the television and just looked at me, waiting quietly.

"You are the most complicated, frustrating, bewitching woman I've ever met. You drive me f-ing crazy, and on so many levels. You are beautiful, funny, brilliant, kooky, unpredictable, ridiculously sexy, mysterious, ridiculously sexy—did I say that already?—moody, harsh, easily distracted, understanding, tough, powerful, scary, respected, irresistible, hyper-critical, uncompromising, generous, well-liked, hard to please, appreciative…"

… and then I lost it. It was the way she was looking at me. Not amused or defensive, but lovingly. Empathetically. Because it was all true, and we both knew it. Or maybe because I was losing it. I felt the lump forming in my throat, right where the words caught and collected, my eyes filling,

213

and then the unthinkable moment for a real man... a tear betrayed me.

We just stared at each other. And then she came to me, sat close, her arms around me, and we just held each other. For the longest time.

It was a moment we will never forget. None of it planned. And my man-card remained unwrinkled.

Ask for feedback, and listen to it.

This may open a can of worms, but if you're ready you may find this conversation to be far more productive than any discussion of your issues has ever been before. If you originate it, you disarm it.

Likewise, when you have feedback to give, ask permission. Ask if the time is right, and if not, you will come back to it later. No tone here, either, that'll sabotage the whole thing. If this is connected to a tough moment between you that leads to an argument, allow enough time to pass before you even think about feedback. Pick a time when all is well. In this moment you are soft, loving... and brave. Your partner won't be able to say no.

Utilize the power of anticipation.

We all like surprises, but we like the sweet anxiety of expectation and mystery even more. Tell your partner to be dressed and ready at a certain time. Tell your partner to pack without saying where you're going. And for a real experience, tell your partner what will happen to them later that evening.

The fun thing is, the two of you get to define what *good* means.

Apologize. Quickly, frequently and sincerely.

Because almost always, no matter how small or trivial, you had a hand in whatever happened.

This, and the tip that comes next, can become a milestone moment in your relationship. It will challenge you to own your stuff, be courageous, and most of all, keep it real. Be honest. For an apology to work it needs to be unconditional, and offered without expecting any form of quid pro quo.

I know several people who have never apologized for anything in their lives. There's a guy like that out there running for president as I write this. It's tough to live with someone like that, because of the oldest and simplest truism on the planet: nobody is perfect.

Do what you have to do. On one side, apologize. On the other, pick your battles and hold your ground when your self-respect demands it.

If there are any unaddressed issues in your recent past—or even your deeper past, though that's a bigger can of domestic worms—sit your partner down and own your end of it. Apologize for what you did wrong, even if it's the subtle stuff, like avoiding talking about it or being insensitive to your partner's point of view.

Leading with an apology, one that is not followed with the word "but..." is a winner every time. It creates the precise context required to get somewhere with the conversation that follows.

It may or may not open a larger conversation. When it does it is almost always a good thing, provided you remain in a vulnerable, humble and open frame of mind. It may evoke a warm hug, which you should appreciate as a breakthrough.

Breakthroughs are the success stories of change.

Another level of apology—this one not specific to something that happened, but rather, something that resides in the air between you—involves defining and owning your role in whatever dysfunction or challenge exists between you. Declare that it hurts you, too. That what you're contributing isn't good enough. That you're done being that person.

My wife came to me, out of the blue, and told me that she apologizes for not saying the things I so often say to her. Explaining that she feels them, but her love language is something else, even though she values my verbal attentiveness greatly. I knew this, I never doubted it, but her hitting the pause button on her day to sit me down and tell me this was a milestone moment. A gift that keeps on giving.

Speaking of hugs… do that.

Often, sincerely, and warmly.

No further explanation needed. Other than this: over a short time, watch how this creates something wonderful between you.

Make a declaration.

You've just defined and owned your end of whatever isn't working in your relationship. The door is now wide open to declare your objectives and intentions going forward. This is a step in creating a new normal between you… beginning with you.

It can be as simple as reversing a few things: instead of being shut off, you'll be open to a new level of vulnerability, intimacy and communications. Declare that you'll be a better communicator, including becoming a better listener, as you move forward together. That you'll strive to keep your partner's point of view and feelings at the forefront of every issue that comes up. Ask your partner to notice, and to hold you accountable to what you're committing to.

Want to be a hero? To play big in this moment? Declare that you'll give your partner the ties. That you no longer need to always be right, or always get your way. Tell your partner that she/he comes first, that you want their life to be calm and warm and anxiety-free. You want it to be full of bliss.

The real value of going there is the process you must endure of bringing these personal truths to the surface. If you can do that—if you can own your stuff—then the primary hurdle to healing and bliss has just been removed, if only for a day.

Be a moment diffuser, not a moment enabler.

Challenges, in the form of irritation, impatience, anger, resentment or hurt feelings, come at us almost every day in a relationship. They don't mean the relationship is in trouble, they are simply part of the equation. A reality we must accept.

It is what we do with these moments that matters.

Sometimes we don't feel we have a choice when it comes to our responses. When the feelings are real, real enough to triumph over a better, more loving choice. Sometimes a touch response is called for. Even in these moments, it is good to live in the pause if you can. To measure and temper your response with love. To come back at it later as your better self.

The worst thing you can when faced with a moment of stress is to escalate. To connect that moment to something recently unresolved, or some *I've-been-meaning-to-talk-to-you-about-this* agenda.

Try not to choose anger and conflict. Try to choose love in these moments, with the long game clearly in mind. If you can truly love your way through them, when the harsher response is more reflex and old tapes than it is warranted, then your road to peace and warmth will be smoother. Or at least, you may not have to go to bed angry and resentful after all.

217

Seize the day.

You might hate me for this. But this is true. I wake up every day and think—and often ask—about what I can do to make my wife's day better. Big or little. Subtle or on-the-nose proactive. Maybe it's me being better about something. Maybe it's me giving her space. Or being less negative and judgmental in general about people and issues that aren't directly about us.

Sometimes, often, the best way for me to add value and light to her day is to simply be a better version—the best possible version—of myself.

It isn't a gesture or a strategy. It is part of our love language. It is how I love her. And it is a *choice*.

My challenge for you, and my hope for you, is to choose well.

Relationships, especially those in recovery, can be very much a one-day-at-a-time proposition. As can the effort to be that best version of yourself. Be there for your partner for each and every one of those days, and you'll round a corner toward a new and better normal.

There's a theme here, which I hope you've noticed. It's about reaching out, being proactive and bold. Even about being creative. About looking into a mirror and asking the tough questions, the answers to many of which you already know. Because one of the reasons relationships go stale is that, over time, it becomes all *about* you. Turn that around and watch the tonality of your relationship take on a new level of positive energy.

I've used the word *normal* frequently here.

Most of the time, it is to assure you that what troubles you may not be unique to your relationship, or in the context of creating a *new normal* between you.

But normal is precisely what I'm *not* asking you to be.

Because when it comes to relationships and love, normal too often dwells somewhere between settling on mediocrity and sucking the life out of you and your partner. One needs only to research divorce statistics, which are dark and depressing, and don't take into account the number of breakups between committed, long term unmarried primary relationships.

What I am asking you to take on, without the slightest hint that it will be easy, is to create a *new* normal between you. For your relationship, and for your life.

I am asking you to choose into the work of getting there, with a full awareness of the degree of difficulty involved. If it were just you, then it would be easier. But it isn't just you. There are two of you. More if you have children in your life. And thus, the math becomes more complex, because while you have access to control over yourself—this, too, is something that life challenges—you have something less than complete control over your partner.

There is great value in acknowledging the differences between you, and honoring them. In taking them into account as life continues to throw you into the blender of day-to-day cohabitation.

Bottom line: the only way you can truly create change in your partner is to implement change within yourself. You may not have to earn their love, but you have to earn their respect, their forgiveness, their partnership and their shared hope.

What have you been doing to earn that respect?

When you can answer that question, the path opens up and the light shines in. Hope returns, unconditional to everything other than the compromise to respect, the limits you have agreed to, authenticity, true friendship, courage and honoring your partner as precisely that: a partner.

If the consequences of bad choices and apathy and depression are indeed the noise between you, a source of guilt and suspicion and resentment, then you need to open up a dialogue about it. And do so without any of the B.S. that contributed to the problems in the first place. If you can't talk it out, find a professional who can help.

The Tough Questions

Stepping into Challenging but Necessary Conversations Between Lovers and Partners Who Are Seeking to Grow as a Couple…

… if You Dare

I've said it several times here… stepping into the process of growth and change requires great courage. Because the status quo is easy, even when it's not.

It bears repeating. Because I am about to test that courage.

Too often there is only one party to the partnership that is questioning the status quo. Probably you, since you are the one reading this. You are the one that is feeling uneasy, because there could be so much more to experience and feel together. Because something may be missing, or broken, or lost, or simply waiting to be discovered.

Too often the conversation doesn't happen because of the fear of repercussions. Your partner isn't comfortable talking in an intimate, challenging context. You fear he/she isn't ready, or willing. Your partner believes that everything is just fine, thank you. Or fine enough.

Or maybe, whatever is broken is your fault, not theirs. You expect resistance, maybe even anger. And when that happens, you'll end up talking about that response, about how you argue, instead of the important issues that are the point in the first place. Instead of talking productively about what needs to happen between you to step onto a path toward greater happiness, a more peaceful tone in your home, less darkness and resentment, more love and affection and an genuine rediscovery of the love you once had, including the passion that came with it.

Or maybe you just don't do this in your relationship. The only time you talk is when you are mending a fence after an argument, and that rarely feels like the best time to open another potentially dramatic can of worms.

When it fact, it may be exactly the right time to go there.

Here are some questions that might make it happen. I won't kid you, these cut deep, and they may make either one of you uncomfortable. But they're also coming straight from the heart of intimacy, which is the context you are seeking to foster.

Intimacy is the agenda.

What happens once these questions are put forth is up to you. My hope is that they take you to a higher place by igniting a new sense of intimacy, honesty and courage between you.

If it's truly too late for things to change between you, if that ship has sailed, then these questions might make that truth painfully apparent. This, too, is a good thing, unless you want to keep living a lie, or you simply are content to compromise.

But if there's an upside waiting to happen, these questions might just throw that switch.

Notice, too, that these inquiries are designed to get your partner talking, rather than creating an opening for you to provide feedback and share your feelings. This is a strategy for disabling any defensiveness, with the hope that the dialogue will become reciprocal through an organic exploration of the deep well of truth and emotion that may bubble up from within it.

Notice if his answers focus on himself, looking inward, or if they are about you. If this becomes a pulpit for him to express his unrest. Which isn't the objective. You are seeking to foster a functional context of becoming more clearly aware of issues so that you might move forward together.

Put your shrink hat on. Look between the lines and notice the framing of the answers. And then, use what you perceive to frame further conversations between you.

Or use them to acknowledge that you, as a couple, may need outside help to identify and resolve the issues between you. A calm discussion is always the place to head in that direction. So make sure this remains a non-confrontational, open and vulnerable discussion between you.

There are no rules here. Just ask. See what happens.

If we could go back in time, would you marry me again? Or, would you choose me again?

How would you describe how I have changed over the years?

How do you believe you have changed since we've been together?

How would you describe how *we* have changed over the years, as a couple?

If you could change something about me, what would that be?

On a scale of one to ten, how happy are you overall, with ten being completely joyful and fulfilled, and one being a complete loss of everything you ever hoped for?

And then, from that... how much of your answer reflects where you and I are today?

What I can do better in our relationship?

What dreams do you still nurture, and how can I help make those happen for you?

Are there any issues between us that are unsettled and unresolved?

How open are you to bringing your true feelings to me? Do I in any way make it feel risky to be completely honest and authentic?

Is there anything you've always wanted to tell me, relative to you and I? How we are doing? How I am acting and being as your partner?

In your mind, are there any apologies I owe you that I haven't offered up?

Are there any sexual fantasies that you have, that you'd like to explore with me? How can I become a better lover for you? How can I make all of your sexual dreams come true?

What's on your bucket list? How can I help make them happen for you, and for us?

What was absolutely our best day together, that you can remember?

Do you have any regrets relative to you and I?

Is there anything I can do to earn back any respect that you may have lost for me over the years?

Do you want to ask me any of these questions, knowing that I'm ready to answer them as honestly, and lovingly, as I can?

You'll know that this is working…

… when your partner turns the tables and asks you to answer the same questions.

Congratulations. You're doing the work. Even if it feels hard, the rewards await, and they'll be worth the effort.

Epilogue

Not long before I finished this book I went in for a regular blood test. The nurse was chatty, and soon we were talking about our respective jobs, hers—with a needle in my arm—being more obvious than mine. When I told her I was a writer, she, like virtually everyone else who hears what I do, asked what I wrote. I said I was writing a book about relationships and the pursuit of bliss. Her face went blank, and she shook her head.

When the needle was removed I showed her the cover. She glanced and less than enthusiastically said, "Cool."

Then she announced that she hated men. That we're all selfish scumbags. I was happy the needle had already been withdrawn from my arm, because it might have been a different experience at this juncture.

She told me about her ex-husband, whom she had divorced three years earlier. She hadn't been out on a date since, which made me sad. She was obviously unhappy and bitter, but doing nothing about it.

Actually, I decided, she was stuck in victim mode.

She said they were very religious. That he used The Bible to support his belief that it was her holy purpose in life to care for him, cooking and cleaning included, to *obey* him, to mind the dog—from this I assumed there were no kids—basically do everything short of mowing the lawn, which was man's work. God said he was the king of his castle, and his role as king was to make a living and to be obeyed.

She was fully employed forty hours a week as a nurse, too, the income from which I assumed he co-opted to fund his love of German cars.

Then, barely drawing a breath, she told me that he had cheated on her. Twice. He was sorry the first time, but then he did it again. He abused her verbally, and one time he shoved her against the wall as he was doing so. He was a big deal in their church. He was golf guy every Saturday, the day she caught up on all the grocery shopping and errands, after which he'd come home snockered. He didn't like to go much of anywhere, didn't do much of anything other than watch television until he fell asleep. His idea of fun was drinking a six pack while watching cable news as she tended to the dishes.

Just like dear old dad, who was probably a flaming asshole, too.

Despite that assumption, I tried not to judge. I know a religious couple whose wife works in the home, *on* the home, and as far as I can tell they're fine. What didn't sit well with me was a man who invoked God's name to license abuse and laziness while he crossed the line of adultery and misogyny.

"How long were you married?" I asked.

"Eleven years."

Now it was my turn to go silent. It wasn't that I couldn't imagine someone remaining with an abusive partner for eleven years, biblical obligation not withstanding. It was the tragedy of it. And the availability of clearer thinking, support and empowerment that was out there if she could only summon the courage to look for it.

In the end, there are always two parties to dysfunction.

I launched into a little lecture about all men not being douchebags—a second term she had used to describe my gender—and maybe if she got out there, she'd find a great guy that wasn't wearing his sphincter as a collar. I offered a litany of some of the things you've just read about here, making sure to flip it to the positive side of relationships, what it takes to live with a man on a fair-and-square basis.

She looked at me and said, "Your wife is very lucky."

I smiled. "Actually, I'm textbook high maintenance. It's me who is the lucky one. But thank you for saying that."

Her last comment on the topic was that she settled for next to nothing in the divorce, because she didn't want to fight him any longer. She just wanted to get away.

That was a Friday. I hadn't fasted for some of the blood tests, so I needed to return, hungry, three days later, on Monday morning. I had thought about her situation all weekend, and I was ready with important things to talk about in the realm of relationship success.

She wasn't there. Her company, which did business within dozens of Walgreen's stores, had shut down the night before. Who goes out of business at ten o'clock PM on a Sunday night?

She was gone. Out of a job.

I had promised her I'd bring in a link to a copy of this manuscript. But there was no way to find her. I hope she departed with some tiny shred of hope. Maybe she can put her experience in a healthier perspective and once again open herself to love.

In the end, I realized both of us were right.

Too often, men *are* douchebags.

Just as often, some women are mistakenly silent in the name of keeping the peace, or fear for her safety, or in many cases, forgetting their own role in contributing toward a joyous, loving, intimate relationship within a tonality of affection and peace that permeates the household. That level of courage is not always easy to summon.

I hope that nurse figures it out. I hope she finds that guy. That she becomes the woman who *will* find that guy.

And I hope, somehow, that she finds this book.

A frightening truth.

Unfortunately, the story of that nurse is not uncommon. Those relational dynamics are the redacted truth of modern domesticity, handed down to us by generation upon generation of unhappiness.

M. Scott Peck was right. Life really is difficult. It is in how we respond to those difficulties that defines not only our destiny, but the very fabric of our character.

Just last night, at the point at which we were finalizing this manuscript, my wife spent time with a friend. She waxed enthusiastically about this material and the way it breaks relationships down into their component pieces so that we might recognize where weak links await. About how to recognize dysfunction so we might address it.

The woman wept. Not for the joy of discovery, but for the inaccessibility of it. She said her husband would never go for any of this. Their marriage is a front. They sleep in separate rooms. He's told her he no longer finds her attractive. He's angry, snapping at people out in the world to the point of confrontation. He refuses to go to counseling, with or without her.

Behold, the prototypical modern dysfunctional male. Basically, he's stuck. Imprisoned behind walls of his own creation.

Many men who were otherwise emotionally functional find themselves in that place soon after they retire. They no longer have a foundational place to go and be, to control, to be needed and experience self-esteem. Their life becomes one long bad mood, hidden behind the most fragile veneer of complacency, cracked open at the slightest provocation.

Women build walls, as well. Ramparts of resentment assembled one snarky brick at a time over years of confrontation, judgement and frustration.

For either gender, the notion of breaking down these walls is daunting. They are bigger and stronger then we are. Too often this forces a default position of simply coping, one of emotional survival in an environment that is no longer safe and no longer fueled by hope.

This is a choice one makes. It doesn't seem like a choice at the time, more like a corner into which one has been painted. Other options are too dark and frightening. To leave and start over, alone, on the back nine of life. Or to confront and invite your partner to engage in some form of therapy, knowing that it won't happen, that the resistance to such a proposition will be immediate and harsh. Perhaps triggering even deeper negativity between you.

This then becomes a significant paradox. To not choose is to elect to simply tough it out, which is, in fact, a choice. To accept that your life will be one of walking on egg shells, waiting for the next bubble of false contentment to burst.

It boils down to three alternatives. First, simply endure. Do your best. Survive. Second, try to open a dialogue, perhaps launched by your announcement that your life together isn't working, and that changes need to be made. And third, get yourselves in front of a professional who can do what you cannot—which is to penetrate the resistance of your partner.

My hope is that you now feel you understand some of the tools that will apply in all three cases. Sooner or later all three choices will have consequences for both of you. Remember, laziness and fear lead to the darkest of those consequences. Courage always opens the higher road.

The journey is a shared one.

My wife, and the experience between us, has been the catalyst that has led me to all that I have learned and believe and have enthusiastically adopted as my way of being, as a husband, a father, a soulmate, a friend, a lover and a domestic partner. It all connects to her in ways that are complex and wondrous. Who she is on both sides of the emotional coin has taught me not just who I must be to move forward, but who I should be to remain with a woman so deserving of the love I heap upon her.

Because what is love, if not the proactive pursuit of your partner's complete happiness, fulfillment, safety and growth on all levels? I ask myself regularly—I take inventory—if I am doing all I can on that front.

It boils down to that. What are you doing to proactively elevate the experience of your partner's life to a higher, more blissful level? And within that question, what might you be doing, however unwittingly as you forge ahead on autopilot, to take away from achieving that level?

The answers to both define your journey, from this point forward.

Actually, they define *you*.

I hope you choose wisely.

The journey is the prize.

My goal is to get away from a win-lose mentality, so common in the marital and partnering dynamic, and step into a more loving place that seeks to give the person with whom we live the win when I can.

My wife has more self-respect than anyone I've ever met. All without the hubris that can come with it. Her limits are clear. Her bar high. Her tolerance for B.S. and the screaming pleas of my inner demons who thrive on it is thin to the point of non-existence. She is highly emotional, prone to extreme reactions, which have tested me and caused me to assume a leadership role in times of stress, even when I am the cause.

And because of her strength and clarity, we have evolved. Neither of us came to our marriage fully formed. We were both possessed of weakness and driven by old tapes and long-expired expectations. Both of us had to unlearn the paradigms of past relationships. Not just about what goes into a successful relationship, but what we must summon from within to stay viable.

On paper, we shouldn't have worked. We are both, to this day, high maintenance.

But we do work. We have grown together. We have chosen. The work remains an everyday proposition, because every day we are nothing more or nothing less than human.

My wish for my son is that he has watched us navigate this journey, and that he has learned from it. His mother found love, too, after her own journey through the darkness. He is 26 as I write this, and hasn't yet found love. Maybe, between the three of us, the adults who raised him, we're part of the reason why. Maybe it all seems like too much work, too much introspective talking.

Because we are not normal. Not remotely.

I wish the same for you. Leave normal behind as you reach for a more joyous way to live. I wish you great bliss as you live out your life in the embrace of empowered and nurturing love. I do this in the knowledge that, while it remains an elusive goal when viewed as a destination without compromise, it is also an experience that comes to us in moments, tiny and finite windows of experience that are linked together to create a baseline tonality.

May your moments of bliss be many, and the sum of them exceeding the richest dreams of happiness you can summon forth.

Play the long game of relationships that work. It won't happen on autopilot, and it won't happen without compromise, patience, tolerance and forgiveness. Nor will it happen without intimacy.

Light the fire again. Fuel it with hope. Find the chemistry that brought you together.

It'll feel like heaven. The keys to which you now possess.

A Word from The Author's Wife

Imagine, if you can, waking up and having your partner ask, "How can I make your day better?"

Twenty-plus years ago I couldn't fathom spending a lifetime with someone that loving and giving. Larry was that way from the beginning of our courtship, and it was he who, simply by being the man he is, changed everything for us.

I'll never forget the look of hurt and disappointment when I occasionally fell into old habits and reacted to my hot buttons, which he often pushed in the beginning, with harshness. There was tone, snappiness, and what he interpreted as disrespect. Often he would react with an expression, as if saying, "I don't deserve to be treated this way."

He didn't.

I am thankful that we survived the consequences. For us, using open communications to work through it, we are stronger because of this awareness. Sexual chemistry doesn't hurt, either.

Those moments were the beginning of change. It takes time to undo old programs, but it can be done. Don't miss the messages by being defensive. Create time for one another that can open a dialogue of authenticity and honesty. If you put your partner first in most things, it comes back to you in the most amazing ways.

Change is hard, and it takes time. But eventually you'll both feel safe and new hope will come to you. If you haven't felt safe in your relationship, I highly recommend you open your heart to these principles to get to that point.

A feeling of safety leads to authenticity, at which point you become more open and vulnerable, which is key to growth. It is truly a journey, one step leading to the next. Intimacy soon follows. And when it leads to the sharing of a dirty little secret, which it absolutely can, it energizes intimacy and sex.

In the past, through his writing and blog posts, Larry has been called arrogant. This is absolutely wrong. What he is, is a humble yet strong and passionate man, the latter coming through in his writing in a way that others too easily misinterpret. I know of no one who is more giving, who cares so deeply about others.

This is where the idea of this book began, with the hope that others might find bliss in their relationship. Or at least take a step or two in that direction.

Imagine the day when you replace the word *when* with *now*. Now I feel safe. Now I feel safe enough to be vulnerable. Now we can share a dirty little secret... now you can go there together.

When you read this, you are alone with it. Nothing is gained by hiding behind a story you've made up that allows you to deal with your reality.

My fear is you won't identify with your shortcomings and inner demons, as we didn't at first. When you can't be wrong you learn nothing because it is through mistakes that we grow. When you are a victim, you fall victim to the blinders you are wearing. When you cannot say you're sorry it implies you can do no wrong, that you think you're perfect... you're not, if nothing else than by virtue of that one thing alone.

I recommend that where the messages in this book ring true, when they apply to *you*, try putting your name in the scenario to better know those weaknesses, to own them and move forward. I hope you become a better person, a better woman and a better man, on this exciting and challenging path. Because of your effort, you almost certainly will.

I wish you the courage that is necessary on the journey to bliss.

After all, isn't love and kindness the true essence of bliss? It really does boil down to something that basic and simple.

Do this work, and you may discover that it is.

Laura Brooks
July 2016

About the Authors

Larry Brooks is the USA Today bestselling author of nine books, including six psychological thrillers (not coincidentally, they deal with, as he puts it, "the way men and women mess with each other's heads in the pursuit of differing agendas, in my stories on the deadly side"), and three #1 bestselling writing books published by Writers Digest Books. He is the creator of the popular fiction writing website, www.storyfix.com, six times named as one of the "101 Best Websites for Writers" (Writers Digest Magazine); he also is on the blogging team at The Kill Zone (www.killzoneblog.com).

Laura Brooks is a retired marketing professional currently pursuing her passion as a painter. This is her first published writing venture, though not her first foray into the realm of human relationships, where she is the go-to resource for family and friends in need of wise council, and, on occasion, comfort ("on occasion" because the truth is not always comforting, and she is a master at boiling truth down to its essence). She frequently reminds friends that she is not The Dark Lady, in reference to the villainess in Larry's first novel, the USA Today bestseller *Darkness Bound*.

Larry and Laura live Scottsdale, Arizona. They have four blended-family children who are old enough to relate to this material (to a great extent, this book is for them), as well as seven grandchildren who aren't. *Chasing Bliss* will be there for them when that time comes.

*****

We hope that this book has touched you in some way. That it helps create awareness that leads to catalyzing and improving your relationship, pointing toward your own definition of bliss.

If it has, even a little, we ask that you recommend this book to people for whom you care. There is no greater gift than sharing a bit of hope, and perhaps the tools to find it. This is the extent of our marketing strategy for this book: the hope that the people it touches might pay it forward.

And, if you are of a mind to, please consider posting a review on Amazon.com, so that others might find their way here.

www.chasingblissbook.com

www.ingramcontent.com/pod-product-compliance
Lightning Source LLC
Chambersburg PA
CBHW061428040426
42450CB00007B/956